D1573279

Effective
Inclusion
Strategies
for Elementary Teachers

Reach and Teach Every Child in Your Classroom

Effective Inclusion Strategies

for Elementary Teachers

Cynthia G. Simpson, Ph.D., Jessica A. Rueter, Ph.D.,
and Jeffrey P. Bakken, Ph.D.

PRUFROCK PRESS INC.
WACO, TEXAS

Library of Congress catalog information
currently on file with the publisher.

Copyright ©2013, Prufrock Press Inc.

Edited by Rachel A. Knox

Cover and layout design by Raquel Trevino

ISBN-13: 978-1-61821-080-7

Printed in the United States of America.

At the time of this book's publication, all facts and figures cited are the most current available. All telephone numbers, addresses, and websites URLs are accurate and active. All publications, organizations, websites, and other resources exist as described in the book, and all have been verified. The authors and Prufrock Press Inc. make no warranty or guarantee concerning the information and materials given out by organizations or content found at websites, and we are not responsible for any changes that occur after this book's publication. If you find an error, please contact Prufrock Press Inc.

Prufrock Press Inc.
P.O. Box 8813
Waco, TX 76714-8813
Phone: (800) 998-2208
Fax: (800) 240-0333
http://www.prufrock.com

Table of Contents

Introduction

Every year, thousands of children begin elementary school, and each enters with his or her own set of attributes and skills. The changing demographics in society and the recent changes to the Individuals with Disabilities Act of 2004 (IDEA) require teachers to instruct students with varying academic levels within the same classroom setting. In fact, many of the students receiving instruction in the general education setting are identified with specific learning disabilities (SLDs). Recent college graduates of teacher preparation programs in the United States have received some instruction in the education of students with disabilities in the general education setting, but changes to federal legislation and the increase in new evidenced-based practices in instructing students in an inclusive classroom make it difficult for teachers to stay abreast of best practices. According to Simpson, Spencer, and Bakken (2011),

> One of the major challenges schools are faced with is making sure that teachers are trained to work in an inclusive setting, which is often made up of students with a wide range of levels of academic and behavioral functioning. (p. 2)

This book helps teachers understand common characteristics of students with specific special needs (see Table 1) and provides specific strategies they can employ in the inclusive classroom setting to meet the needs of these learners. However, this book is not all-inclusive and many additional resources and website references are located throughout the book to provide readers with more in-depth information about the current topics.

Successful Inclusion Strategies for Elementary Teachers provides both general and special education teachers with a guide for working collaboratively in meeting the needs of students with disabilities in the inclusive classroom. The authors recognize that the background of the reader and the experience gained throughout a teacher's career will impact the way this book is used. However, it is the authors' intent that the book serve as a resource to all teachers working with students with special needs. The materials presented are based on best practices in the field of special education and use person-first language (e.g., *children with learning disabilities* instead of *learning disabled children*).

Chapter 1 surveys the laws that impact the instruction of students in the inclusive classroom. The Individuals with Disabilities Act of 2004 (IDEA), Americans with Disabilities Act (ADA), and Section 504 of the Rehabilitation Act of 1973 are discussed in this chapter. Chapter 2 introduces the reader to the inclusive classroom with a brief description of how to structure an inclusive classroom and characteristics of effective inclusive classrooms, including the following characteristics identified in *Successful Inclusion Strategies for Early Childhood Teachers* (Simpson & Warner, 2010):

- Inclusive classrooms have at least one child with a special need. In preschool classrooms, children with special needs are not always identified.
- The classroom should not have more than 10% of its students identified as having special needs.
- Teachers in inclusive classrooms should have a strong background in child development principles and recognize that development occurs over time and is different for every child. Consequently, teachers should continually assess various aspects of the inclusive classroom. This includes making decisions about room arrangement, reviewing classroom instruction, and working with families, as well as assessing children's developmental progress to maximize each child's learning potential.
- Teachers organize instruction in order to meet children's needs as a group and as individuals. When instructing the group, teachers adjust their plans to accommodate for any child with a disability.
- Teachers plan instruction so that children, regardless of their development, will have activities that provide opportunities for them to develop confidence and competence in learning as well as experience appropriate challenges. The design of appropriate and inclusive learning experiences

Table 1

COMMON CHARACTERISTICS OF CHILDREN WITH SPECIFIC SPECIAL NEEDS

Special Need	Characteristics
Students With Autism Spectrum Disorder	◆ Develop language differently than most children (most often delayed) ◆ Experience minimum social development (not spontaneous) ◆ Often participate in repetitive behaviors (such as echolalia, the repetition of sounds) ◆ Often exhibit disruptive behavior (especially in classrooms) ◆ Are highly sensitive to sensory experiences and movement ◆ Demonstrate irregular intellectual development (unusual patterns of strengths and weaknesses)
Students With Attention Deficit/ Hyperactivity Disorder (ADHD)	◆ Show inattentive behavior ◆ Exhibit hyperactive and impulsive behaviors ◆ Experience difficulty in relationships with adults and peers ◆ Often have low self-esteem
Students With Speech and/ or Language Impairments	◆ Possess disorders that affect the rate and rhythm of speech ◆ Often cannot produce various sounds ◆ Often omit or add sounds when producing words ◆ Often distort sounds ◆ May have voice disorders, such as an unusually high pitch or nasality (when sounds seem to be emitted through children's noses) ◆ May possess limited ability to express themselves (language impairment) ◆ May experience difficulty following directions or understanding verbal emotions (language impairment)
Students With Hearing Impairments	◆ Often ignore adults and/or peers when they are spoken to ◆ May exhibit confusion when responding to questions or instructions ◆ Often cannot hear unless they are facing the speaker ◆ Often demonstrate unclear language production ◆ Often struggle with social behaviors ◆ May be unable to hear in a noisy classroom (sensory defensiveness)
Students With Vision Impairments	◆ Have impairments ranging from minor deficits to total blindness ◆ May experience different levels of eye function from day to day ◆ Are visually affected by classroom lighting, time of day, and weather ◆ May be hypersensitive to touch (tactile defensiveness) ◆ May have other disabilities (up to 60% of children with visual impairments do) ◆ Tend to rely on nonverbal senses to receive information
Students With Orthopedic Impairments (Physical Impairments)	◆ May have a congenital condition ◆ May have cerebral palsy, spina bifida, muscular dystrophy, and/or fractures or burns; orthopedic impairments vary widely depending on the specific type of orthopedic impairment (congenital conditions or as a result of accidents) ◆ May experience paralysis, tightness or weakness in the legs or throughout the body, or chronic inflammation and pain of the joints ◆ May or may not have a learning disability
Students With Specific Learning Disabilities	◆ May have issues with organization (e.g., in writing, personal life, completing work) ◆ Often struggles with reading comprehension ◆ Demonstrates poor memory (e.g., for vocabulary, facts in any subject, word meanings, math facts, letter formation) ◆ May struggle with writing (e.g., poor sentence structure, sloppy presentation, wrong punctuation) ◆ Has trouble problem solving (in any subject or in personal situations) ◆ Has difficulty performing multiple steps in a sequence (both academically and socially) ◆ Demonstrates poor social skills (e.g., struggles with asking questions, asking for help, realizing they need help, accepting help)

Table 1, continued

Special Need	Characteristics
Students With Traumatic Brain Injury	• May have experienced an external physical injury • Have difficulty gaining educational achievement • May exhibit motor dysfunction • Often have problems with attention and memory • May have difficulties in communicating with others • May exhibit social and emotional changes

Note. Adapted from *Successful Inclusion Strategies for Early Childhood Teachers* (p. xii) by C. G. Simpson and L. Warner, 2010, Waco, TX: Prufrock Press. Copyright 2010 Prufrock Press. Adapted with permission.

helps children feel good about what they are learning, but also challenges them to move to higher levels of knowledge acquisition.

◻ Teachers document learning for all children in the classroom using assessment strategies that meet the needs of the children's ages, individual needs, and growth.

◻ Inclusive classrooms maintain regular contact with families and service providers (such as speech therapists, intervention specialists, and other professionals who work with children with special needs).

◻ Children in inclusive classrooms learn together regardless of their differences and abilities. Their opportunities to interact give all children invaluable experiences with others who may learn or interact in different ways.

◻ Inclusive classrooms are a microcosm of the larger society. When children with special needs enter classrooms, they are given the chance to adjust to real-world activities that they will need to understand when they become adults. Likewise, young children learn to accept others who are different and develop respect for all children. (pp. xiv–xv)

Chapters 3–11 each begin with a specific vignette that illustrates a typical situation a teacher may encounter in his or her classroom when instructing students with an identified special need. Students described within the text are actual students, and the scenarios are taken from real-life situations. However, no two students are alike, and each student identified with a disability will manifest the characteristics of the disability in his or her unique way. This text focuses on the most commonly occurring disabilities in the elementary school setting: autism spectrum disorder, Attention Deficit/Hyperactivity Disorders (ADHD; not identified under IDEA as one of the 13 disability areas but often recognized in the public school system as Other Health Impaired), learning disabilities, emotional/behavioral disorders, speech and language disorders, hearing impairments, visual impairments, orthopedic impairments (physical impairments), and intellectual disabilities. In addition to the scenarios presented, Chapters 3–11 each include an overview of a specific disability, what elementary school teachers need to know about the disability, and information about particular strategies, interventions, and services (see Table 2) teachers employed when working with the particular student described in the opening scenario.

The last three chapters (Chapters 12–14) address other topics that can impact elementary school teachers. Chapter 12 examines how assistive technology can be implemented to support students with disabilities in reading, writing, and mathematics, as well as organization and self-management. The chapter also looks at different types and legal aspects of assistive technology. Chapter 13 addresses the very important topic of collaborating with students' families. It presents different types of parents and families, the impact of culture and heritage, and different ways to get parents and families involved with the teacher and school to become an integral part of the education of their child. Chapter 14 explores Response to Intervention (RtI), how it can impact the education of all students, and how it impacts the inclusive classroom teacher.

Teachers should recognize that they can make enormous differences in a student's life. It is important to look at the whole child, as it is easy to focus only on managing or ameliorating disabilities. Teachers can find out what student's strengths and interests are and emphasize them and create opportunities for success in the classroom.

Table 2
RELATED SERVICES AND THEIR PURPOSES

Related Service	General Purposes
Speech or language pathology (See http://www.asha.org)	For identification, diagnosis, or appraisal of communication disorders. For treatment or counseling for communication disorders. For pragmatic, or social, language disorders. For listening, following directions, or expressing oneself. For prevention of communication disorders.
Transportation	For travel to and from school, usually door to door.
Audiology services (http://www.asha.org)	For hearing loss or deafness.
Interpreting services	For transcription, signing for children who are deaf or hard of hearing, technological transcription, and special transcription for children who are deaf and blind.
Psychological services	For development of positive behavior supports and strategies, counseling, consultation, assessment, and training.
Physical therapy (http://www.apta.org)	For gross motor and other motor problems. For physical movement and activity.
Occupational therapy (http://www.aota.org)	For functional independence, through skills provided by a qualified occupational therapist. For preventing or limiting impairment of functional activities.
Transition services	For a coordinated set of activities to develop achievement and functional performance, to allow the child movement from school to postschool activities.
Travel training	For students with cognitive disabilities, who need instruction in awareness of the environment and how to get from place to place in the school or community.
Recreation; therapeutic recreation	For leisure skills assessment, leisure education, therapeutic recreation services, or recreation programs and services.
Early identification and assessment	For assurance that a plan to identify a child's disability is found and addressed as early as possible.
Social work services (http://www.socialworkers.org)	For counseling or other mental health direct or indirect services. Services provided by a licensed or otherwise qualified social worker.
School health services	For medication at school, collaboration with prescribing doctor, medical monitoring, or monitoring of medication effect in classroom, when nurse or other health professional is a required member of an MDT. Can be delivered by a nurse or other qualified personnel.
Counseling services	For guidance counseling, social skills counseling, or other counseling. Provided by social workers, guidance counselors, psychologists, or otherwise qualified professionals.

Note. From *School Success for Kids With Emotional and Behavioral Disorders* (pp. 187–188) by M. R. Davis, V. P. Culotta, E. A. Levine, and E. H. Rice, 2011, Waco, TX: Prufrock Press. Copyright 2011 Prufrock Press. Reprinted with permission.

Overview of Educational Laws That Affect Inclusive Classrooms

All teachers should possess a basic understanding of the laws that impact students with disabilities in inclusive classrooms. This chapter provides an overview of The Individuals with Disabilities Education Act (2004), No Child Left Behind Act (2001), and two civil rights laws, (Section 504 of the Rehabilitation Act of 1973 and the Americans with Disabilities Act [1990]). Figure 1 illustrates the major laws applying to special education eligibility.

HISTORICAL OVERVIEW

Since the late 1950s, the federal government has been involved in the education of students with disabilities. Some of the early laws included the Education of Mentally Retarded Children Act of 1958 and the Training of Professional Personnel Act of 1959. In 1965, President Lyndon Johnson signed into law the Elementary and Secondary Education Act (ESEA). This law was the first in which states received federal funding to assist in educating a certain group of students. The purpose of ESEA was to provide federal money to states to improve educational opportunities for children who were disadvantaged, including students

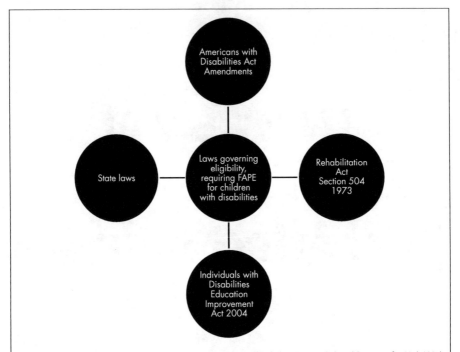

Figure 1. Major laws applying to special education eligibility. From *School Success for Kids With Emotional and Behavioral Disorders* (p. 158) by M. R. Davis, V. P. Culotta, E. A. Levine, and E. H. Rice, 2011, Waco, TX: Prufrock Press. Copyright 2011 Prufrock Press. Reprinted with permission.

with disabilities who attended state schools for the deaf, blind, and intellectually disabled (Yell, 2006).

On November 29, 1975, President Gerald Ford signed into law the Education for All Handicapped Children Act (EAHCA). This act is popularly known as P.L. 94-142 and was the first law that guaranteed students with disabilities a right to a free and appropriate public education (FAPE; Smith, 2001). Prior to 1975, students with disabilities had little to no access to educational opportunities. In fact, many students with disabilities were completely excluded from public schools, and those that attended public schools did not receive an appropriate education to meet their needs. The passage of P.L. 94-142 opened the doors of schools for students with disabilities (Bowen & Rude, 2006).

P.L. 94-142 has been amended several times since being enacted in 1975. In 1990, P.L. 94-142 was renamed the Individuals with Disabilities Education Act (IDEA). This amendment added two disability categories, autism and traumatic brain injury, and substituted the word *disability* for *handicap* throughout the law. The law also emphasized the use of person-first language. For example, the law uses "student with a disability" rather than "disabled student," putting the person before the disability (Yell, 2006). In 1997, Congress once again amended IDEA. One of the hallmarks of the 1997 reauthorization was a specific focus on accountability and assessment practices (Sack-Min, 2007). In particular, the reauthorization of 1997 mandated that schools demonstrate measurable improvements in the educational achievements of students with disabilities (Yell, 2006). Also added was the area of transition. Starting at age 14, all students with disabilities must be involved in planning for after high school. Parents and the student, along with the special education teacher, are involved in this process.

The most recent amendment of P.L. 94-142 occurred in 2004 when George W. Bush signed the Individuals with Disabilities Education Improvement Act (IDEA, 2004) into law. The changes in IDEA 2004 were substantial: there were changes in the Individualized Education Program (IEP), discipline, and identification of students with learning disabilities (Yell, 2006). IDEA 2004 was also the first time that the education of students with disabilities would be held to the same high standards as their nondisabled peers (Sack-Min, 2007). There's no longer any debate over whether students with disabilities should have access to a classroom. Now IDEA's focus has shifted from access to accountability to ensuring that students with disabilities receive a quality education and show academic progress (Sack-Min, 2007, p. 2).

Following are important principles for school districts to understand and comply with to ensure that they meet the requirements of IDEA and provide educational benefit for students with disabilities (Yell, Ryan, Rozalski, & Katsiyannis, 2009):

- Principle 1: Ensure that parents are meaningfully involved in the development of their children's special education program.
- Principle 2: Ensure that teachers and administrators understand their responsibilities under the FAPE requirements of IDEA.
- Principle 3: Ensure that special education teachers understand how to develop educationally meaningful and legally sound IEPs.
- Principle 4: Ensure that special education administrators and teachers receive meaningful and sustained in-service training programs in new research-based practices and other developments in special education. (p. 74–75)

Under this revision, general education teachers are to be a part of the IEP process. For a student to be eligible for services under IDEA, he or she must meet the criteria for eligibility in one or more of the 13 disability categories and demonstrate an adverse impact on educational performance. In addition, several questions must be answered for eligibility under IDEA. See Table 3 and Figure 2.

Table 3
SPECIAL EDUCATION CATEGORIES

Category	Definition
Autism	A developmental disability significantly affecting verbal and nonverbal communication and social interaction, generally evident before age 3
Deafness	A hearing impairment that is so severe that the child is impaired in processing linguistic information, with or without amplification
Deaf-blindness	Simultaneous hearing and visual impairments
Hearing impairment	An impairment in hearing, whether permanent or fluctuating
Intellectual disabilities (mental retardation)	Significantly subaverage general intellectual functioning existing concurrently with deficits in adaptive behavior
Multiple disabilities	The manifestation of two or more disabilities (such as intellectual disabilities-blindness), the combination of which requires special accommodation for maximal learning
Orthopedic impairment	Physical disabilities, including congenital impairments, impairments caused by disease, and impairments from other causes
Other health impairment	Having limited strength, vitality, or alertness due to chronic or acute health problems; includes Attention Deficit/Hyperactivity Disorder
Serious emotional disturbance	A disability where a child of typical intelligence has difficulty, over time and to a marked degree, building satisfactory interpersonal relationships; responds inappropriately behaviorally or emotionally under normal circumstances; demonstrates a pervasive mood of unhappiness; or has a tendency to develop physical symptoms or fears
Specific learning disability	A disorder in one or more of the basic psychological processes involved in understanding or in using language, spoken or written, which may manifest itself in an imperfect ability to listen, think, speak, read, write, spell, or do mathematical calculations
Speech or language impairment	A communication disorder such as stuttering, impaired articulation, a language impairment, or a voice impairment
Traumatic brain injury	An acquired injury to the brain caused by an external physical force, resulting in total or partial functional disability, psychosocial impairment, or both
Visual impairment	A visual difficulty (including blindness) that, even with correction, adversely affects a child's educational performance

From Maryville City Schools (2005). *Note.* From *Teacher's Survival Guide: The Inclusive Classroom* (p. 49) by C. G. Simpson, V. G. Spencer, and J. P. Bakken, 2011, Waco, TX: Prufrock Press. Copyright 2011 Prufrock Press. Reprinted with permission.

ATTENTION DEFICIT HYPERACTIVITY DISORDER

With particular respect to attention deficit/hyperactivity disorders (ADHD), in 1990 Congress required the United States Department of Education to issue a policy memorandum stating that students with ADHD be served under Other Health Impairments (OHI) category provided they demonstrate problems specifically associated with alertness, vitality, or strength that negatively impact educa-

Figure 2. Questions that must be answered for eligibility under IDEA. From *School Success for Kids With Emotional and Behavioral Disorders* (p. 159) by M. R. Davis, V. P. Culotta, E. A. Levine, and E. H. Rice, 2011, Waco, TX: Prufrock Press. Copyright 2011 Prufrock Press. Reprinted with permission.

| Attention Deficit Disorder or Attention Deficit/Hyperactivity Disorder (ADD/ADHD) |
| Predominantly Hyperactive-Impulsive Type (sometimes called ADHD-PHI) |
| Predominantly Inattentive Type (sometimes called ADHD-PI) |
| Combined Type (sometimes called ADHD-C) |

Figure 3. Types of ADHD (Spodak & Stefano, 2011).

tional performance. A student may also qualify for services if he or she meets the criteria for other disabilities, such as a learning disability. That is, a student can be diagnosed with ADHD and categorized as having a learning disability (Reid & Katsiyannis, 1995). To clarify further, ADHD does not have a specific eligibility category under IDEA. Rather, if a child meets the eligibility criteria of ADHD, he or she may be served under the Other Health Impairments category. For the purposes of this text, each of the types of ADHD (see Figure 3) will be addressed.

CIVIL RIGHTS LEGISLATION

In 1973, Congress passed the Rehabilitation Act of 1973 (Public Law [P.L.] 93-112). Section 504 of this Act was the first federal civil rights law to protect the rights of persons with disabilities. The intent of Section 504 is to prohibit discrimination against a person with a disability by any agency that received federal funding (Smith, 2001; Yell, 2006). It requires that school districts provide FAPE to qualified students in their jurisdictions. (Qualified students have a physical or mental impairment that substantially limits one or more major life activities regardless of the nature or severity of the disability.) Under Section 504, FAPE requires schools to provide regular or special education and related aids and services designed to meet the student's individual educational needs as adequately as the needs of nondisabled students are met. Section 504 is one more way that students with disabilities can get the services they need to be successful in school or work environments.

AMERICANS WITH DISABILITIES ACT

A related civil rights law is the Americans with Disabilities Act (ADA) of 1990. ADA applies to all entities in the United States, regardless of whether they receive federal funds or not. The only two entities exempted from ADA are churches and private clubs. Thus, private schools that do not receive federal funding (and are therefore exempt from Section 504) are not exempt from ADA requirements. ADA specifically requires that reasonable accommodations or modifications be made to ensure persons with disabilities have access to goods and services (Smith, 2001).

Even though Section 504 and ADA are civil rights laws, they have a direct and substantial impact on educational programming and services for students with disabilities. They both provide opportunities for students with disabilities free from discrimination based on that disability. They also grant students certain privileges just like students without disabilities. For example, students with disabilities could receive their education in regular classrooms, education in regular classes with supplementary services, and/or special education with related services. Therefore, general education teachers need to be aware of the legal guidelines for identification, eligibility, and evaluation of students with disabilities in their classrooms (deBettencourt, 2002).

SUMMARY OF DIFFERENCES BETWEEN SECTION 504 AND IDEA

Not all students with disabilities are protected under IDEA. Those children who are not protected under IDEA are protected under Section 504. To be eligible under Section 504, an identified physical or mental condition must substantially limit a major life activity. Examples of major life activities include walking, seeing, hearing, speaking, breathing, learning, working, and caring for oneself. Schools may offer less assistance and monitoring to Section 504 students because there are fewer federal government regulations instructing schools to do so, especially as it relates to compliance (deBettencourt, 2002).

In contrast, to be protected under IDEA, students must meet the following two requirements: specific eligibility requirements and adverse impact on educational performance (Yell, 2006). Section 504 covers the lifespan and provides safeguards for persons with disabilities in many aspects of their lives (e.g., employ-ment, public access to buildings, transportation, and education), whereas IDEA requires states to provide services for children with disabilities from ages 3–21 (deBettencourt, 2002).

The 504 plan and the Individualized Education Program (IEP) are both learning plans for students with disabilities; however, there are some major differ-ences between them. The 504 plan offers all children with disabilities equal access to an education, while the IEP is only for children who require special education services. The IEP document must be individualized to meet each child's unique needs while also promoting an educational benefit to the student. The IEP docu-ments contain very specific language and information—such as goals, objectives, and timelines—that is not included in the 504 plan. The 504 plan is documented in a written plan but is not specific. Furthermore, when a 504 plan is developed, there are no requirements stating who must attend the 504 plan meeting. An IEP meeting, however, requires a minimum number of IEP participants (e.g., administrator, general education teacher, and special education teacher). If a 504 plan is not being followed, the Office for Civil Rights of the U.S. Department of Education needs to be contacted. For noncompliance of an IEP, the request must be made to the state's Department of Education. Finally, the 504 plan does not offer as many specific procedural safeguards as the IEP. For example, a procedural safeguard for the IEP is the right to request an independent assessment at the public's expense. See Figure 4 for a comparison of the 504 plan and the IEP.

NO CHILD LEFT BEHIND ACT

On January 8, 2002, President George W. Bush signed into law the No Child Left Behind Act (NCLB). The law's primary purpose was to improve student achievement. The law required that states establish rigorous systems for measur-ing students' performance while holding school districts and schools accountable for their outcomes (Yell, 2006). Included in NCLB was the requirement that all students score at the "proficient" level on state assessments by 2013–2014 (NCLB, 2001). The focus of NCLB was on high-stakes assessment created to incentivize or punish districts and schools based on students' performance (Simpson, LaCava, & Graner, 2004). The key provisions of NCLB are accountability, use of scientif-ically based instruction, and highly qualified personnel.

Under the provisions of NCLB, students with disabilities are included in the accountability requirements of NCLB. Specifically, students with disabilities must be assessed and the results reported to determine if the school and district meet the accountability requirements under the law (Yell, 2006). Schools argue

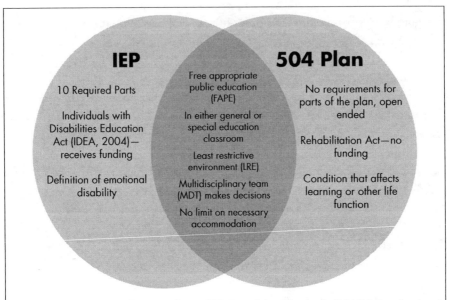

Figure 4. A comparison of the 504 plan and IEP. From *School Success for Kids With Emotional and Behavioral Disorders* (p. 199) by M. R. Davis, V. P. Culotta, E. A. Levine, and E. H. Rice, 2011, Waco, TX: Prufrock Press. Copyright 2011 Prufrock Press. Reprinted with permission.

that this process isn't fair if the school has a large population of students with disabilities. If this is the case, the scores of the entire school may not be totally reflective of the population that attends.

ELEMENTARY EDUCATION SPECIAL EDUCATION SETTINGS

Special education services occur in a variety of settings in elementary schools. Individualized Education Program committee members must consider the least restrictive environment (LRE) to the maximum extent possible, and, accordingly, the LRE will vary with the needs of each individual child (see Figure 5). The IEP team can consider a variety of placement options, such as a general education setting with supports (i.e., co-teaching and inclusion services), general education with pull-out programs, resource rooms, separate classes with general education activities/content, and self-contained/separate classes. The general education setting with co-teaching services and/or inclusion services is the least specialized and least separate, whereas self-contained classes are the most restrictive and most separate (Simpson et al., 2011).

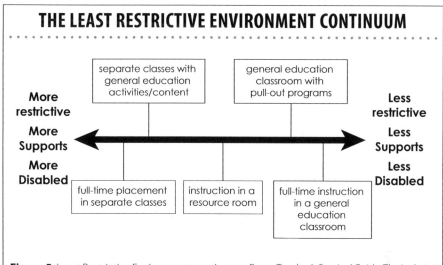

Figure 5. Least Restrictive Environment continuum. From *Teacher's Survival Guide: The Inclusive Classroom* (p. 57) by C. G. Simpson, V. G. Spencer, and J. P. Bakken, 2011, Waco, TX: Prufrock Press. Copyright 2011 Prufrock Press. Reprinted with permission.

CONFIDENTIALITY AND PRIVACY

Students with disabilities have records related to special education programming, including eligibility status, sociological and family information, and educational placements that are protected under IDEA and the Family Education Rights and Privacy Act (FERPA). When accessing a student's special education file, only those individuals who have a specific need to know (e.g., the student's teachers, administrators, and special education personnel) may do so. School districts are required to keep a written log of who accesses each file and why.

Parents of children with disabilities also have the right to inspect and review their child's education records. Parental access includes the right to have information in the child's eligibility file explained or interpreted and the right to obtain copies of the records. Usually, information from the child's special education records may not be released without parental consent. However, information may be released to participating agencies without parental consent in order to comply with IDEA. For example, when a child moves from one district to another, the receiving district will need a copy of the child's current IEP to provide appropriate services to the child, and schools can transfer this information without parental consent.

DISCIPLINE

When determining the appropriate disciplinary actions for students with disabilities, schools may follow the same discipline procedures they use with students who are not disabled with a few exceptions. Schools may suspend or expel a student with a disability for up to 10 days. After the 10th day of removal, schools must hold a manifestation determination review meeting to determine if the behavior is a manifestation of the student's disability. If a determination is made that no relationship exists between the behavior and the disability, the same disciplinary procedures that occur for students without disabilities may be imposed on the student with a disability. In these cases, educational services are continued as written in the student's IEP.

In certain instances, school officials may remove a student to an alternative educational setting for 45 school days, regardless of whether the behavior is a result of the disability. There are three reasons that unilateral removal for 45 school days occur: (1) the student brings a weapon to school or a school function; (2) the student possesses, uses, or sells drugs or controlled substances during school or at a school function; or (3) if it is substantially likely that the student will cause serious bodily injury to self or others and provided that the school officials have made reasonable efforts to minimize risk of such injury.

IMPLICATIONS OF FEDERAL LAWS ON INCLUSIVE CLASSROOMS

The Individuals with Disabilities Education Act (2004) and Section 504 specifically stipulate that schools receiving federal funds must comply with the legal requirements to provide services for students with disabilities. Further, as momentum grows for students with disabilities to have access to general education curriculum, school personnel must understand inclusive classroom practices. Provided below are suggestions for elementary school educators who teach children with disabilities in inclusive classroom settings:

  ◻ *Understand federal legislation:* Section 504 and IDEA both mandate that schools provide services for all children with disabilities. Further, IDEA stipulates that children receive a free and appropriate public education in the least restrictive environment possible, which means that students with disabilities should be educated with their nondisabled peers to the maximum extent possible. That is, students with disabilities can only be placed in separate classes or special schools when the severity of their disabilities are such that they cannot receive a free appropriate public education in the general education classroom even when provided with supplementary aids and services (IDEA, 2004). This mandate ensures that schools educate students with disabilities alongside students with and without disabilities to the maximum extent possible (Yell, 2006).

¤ *Use universal design models when designing classroom activities and lessons:* Universal Design for Learning (UDL) assists teachers in recognizing that inflexible instructional techniques and curricular materials are barriers to diverse learners just as stairs are barriers for people who have physical disabilities. When designing curricula, teachers must recognize the variety of diverse learners in their classrooms and build in options to support learning from the very beginning (Hitchcock, Meyer, Rose, & Jackson, 2002). UDL curriculum offers an array of options for accessing, using, and engaging with the learning materials. Accordingly, the UDL model emphasizes that no single approach will work for all students (Rose & Meyer, 2002) and leads to the development of flexible instructional techniques and curriculum that can support all learners more efficiently (Hitchcock et. al, 2002). It requires that teachers consider all students when designing classroom activities and lessons:

> Although educators will always need to modify and adapt the environment to meet the individual needs of some students, the Universal Design model can establish a foundation for likely success from which teachers can later address the particular needs of individual students. (Stockall, Dennis, & Miller, 2012, p. 10)

¤ *Understand coteaching models:* Generally, inclusive classrooms provide a framework for special education teachers and/or paraprofessionals to teach alongside the general education teacher. As with any instructional methodology, there are best practices in providing coteaching services. In particular, there are six generally accepted coteaching models that can be implemented in an inclusive setting: One Teach, One Assist; Team Teaching; Parallel Teaching; One Teach, One Monitor; Alternative Teaching; and Station Teaching (Ploessl, Rock, Schoenfeld, & Blanks, 2010). All parties involved must understand the nuances of each of the particular models and must consider the needs of the children when implementing a particular coteaching model. In other words, no one model will work in every situation or with every lesson.

¤ *Collaborate:* Teachers must collaborate with one another in order to meet the needs of students who have disabilities in their classrooms. It is critical that general education teachers and special education teachers work together in providing educational opportunities, activities, and lessons specifically designed to address unique learning needs. Further, children with special needs sometimes require related services such as occupational therapy, physical therapy, or special transportation. In these cases, it is vital that the classroom teacher collaborate with the related personnel in providing services according to the child's IEP.

¤ *Form relationships with families*: IDEA requires parental participation in evaluation, IEP meetings, and placement decisions. The goal is to have parents play a significant and meaningful role in the education of their children (Yell, 2006). It is incumbent upon educators to form relationships with families to ensure that parental participation occurs. Moreover, parents know their children best and can provide insight into what may or may not work in the school environment. The relationships that educators form with families will help support their children in a variety of academic settings.

CONCLUSION

Laws in special education are in a constant state of change. Thus, it is important that educators who teach students with disabilities keep abreast of the changes in the laws. IDEA was designed to protect the rights of students with disabilities and ensure access to the general education curriculum, but it also protects school districts and the teachers serving students with disabilities. Understanding the basic principles of IDEA, Section 504, and ADA will assist teachers in the inclusive classroom to provide the best services that they can to students with disabilities and their families.

IF YOU WANT TO KNOW MORE

American with Disabilities Act—http://www.ada.gov
Office of Special Education and Rehabilitative Services—http://www2.ed.gov/about/offices/list/osers/osep/index.html
Wrights Law—http://wrightslaw.com

2

The Inclusive Classroom

Alex is an elementary student in the second grade and has been diagnosed with a learning disability in the area of reading. Alex has received pull-out services with a reading specialist to improve his reading abilities, but at a recent IEP meeting, the members agreed that Alex would be served best in the general education classroom.

Mr. Roland is Alex's teacher. He is worried that Alex will not make the gains he needs in order to perform at grade-level standards. Moreover, Mr. Roland is concerned about how he will provide the intensive reading instruction that Alex requires to master his IEP goals and objectives. To address his concerns, the IEP team agreed that Ms. Simmons, Alex's special education teacher, will provide coteaching services in Mr. Roland's classroom. This arrangement will require Mr. Roland and Ms. Simmons to collaboratively work together so that Alex can benefit from the instructional process.

More and more students with disabilities are being educated in general education classrooms. Therefore, it is vital that best practices for including students with disabilities are adopted by the professionals that work within these environments. This chapter provides an overview of inclusion and best practices of inclusive classrooms.

OVERVIEW OF INCLUSION

Inclusion is the education of students with disabilities with their typically developing peers and with special education supports and services provided as necessary to meet their needs. Although not required by law, inclusionary practices are one way that the least restrictive environment can be met. The key principle of inclusion is shared responsibility by general and special educators for students with disabilities (Vaughn, Bos, & Schumm, 2011).

Inclusion is not a place or a classroom setting. Rather, it is a philosophy of including students in a community of learners. As such, it suggests that students with disabilities belong to and are valued members of the community. In the general education classroom, they are given supports that offer them the opportunity to succeed (McLeskey, Rosenberg, & Westling, 2013).

Least Restrictive Environment

Inclusion is supported by the least restrictive environment (LRE) mandate in the Individuals with Disabilities Education Act (2004). The LRE requires schools to educate children with disabilities as much as possible with their typically-developing peers. Accordingly, the LRE will vary with the needs of each student and should be individually determined. Thus, the LRE for one student will not be the LRE for another student. Moreover, students who are not successful in general education classrooms when provided with supports and when it is determined that a separate class can be more beneficial can be moved to a more restrictive environment (McLeskey et al., 2013).

To implement the LRE, IDEA requires that school districts use the continuum of placement options (i.e., continuum of services) for students with disabilities. The continuum of placement options provides a framework from which the LRE can be implemented, and options range from an integrated setting, such as a general education class with supports, to highly segregated settings where services are provided in hospitals and residential facilities (Salend, 2011; Simpson et al., 2011).

There has been much debate regarding the efficacy of inclusion and its benefit for students with disabilities. Research does not support one service delivery model over another. In other words, the setting in which services are delivered is not as important as the quality of the instructional practices that are implemented. Decisions regarding placement must be determined with respect to the instructional practices that enable the student to meet his or her individual goals and objectives (Zigmond, 2003). Thus, it is critical that the continuum of placement options be evaluated carefully when determining a student's least restrictive environment.

When considering inclusion services for students with disabilities, responsible inclusionary practices are critical to ensure success for these students. Guidelines for responsible inclusion include the following elements:

- The student comes first. The key objective is the extent to which the child makes academic and/or social gains.
- Inclusive classrooms receive adequate materials and personnel.
- A continuum of placement options is considered and maintained.
- The delivery model in which services are implemented is evaluated regularly with respect to the student's academic and social needs.
- Educators receive ongoing professional development on effective instructional practices that can be implemented in the least restrictive environment.
- Curricula and instructional practices meet the needs of all students in the least restrictive environment. (Vaughn et al., 2011)

Teaching in Inclusive Schools

As more and more students with disabilities are included in general education settings, general and special educators share in the responsibility of providing instruction for these students. The degree to which inclusive services are successfully implemented depends on teachers' attitudes toward inclusion and the ability to collaborate with others. Idol (2006) reported that there was a trend among educators toward including students with disabilities in general education classroom. Few teachers participating in this study chose self-contained special education classes as the preferred choice for delivery of services. Administrators in this study also supported inclusionary practices as long as adequate resources and personnel were provided and that the personnel in inclusive settings could work with any student needing assistance rather than only with students who had disabilities. Moreover, when inclusive programs are well-designed, teachers tend to be supportive of having students with disabilities in general education classrooms (McLeskey et al., 2013).

Collaboration

The ability for teachers to collaborate with one another is a critical component to successful inclusive classrooms. Friend and Cook (2007) defined interpersonal collaboration as "a style for direct interaction between at least two co-equal parties voluntarily engaged in shared decision making as they work toward a common goal" (p. 7). In particular, collaboration is the nature of the interpersonal relationship that occurs during the interaction and the ways in which participants communicate with each other. According to Friend and Cook (2007), key elements of successful collaboration are:

- Collaboration is voluntary. Inclusive classrooms work well when the educators involved voluntarily collaborate with one another in their interactions. In a review of the literature, Pugach and Winn (2011) noted that when teachers volunteered for coteaching, they were more satisfied than those who did not volunteer and that the volunteers reported increased mutual respect for their coteacher than those who did not volunteer.
- Collaboration requires equal contribution among participants. Interactions are valued and each person has equal power in decision making.
- Collaboration is based on mutual goals. Individuals who collaborate must share at least one mutual goal.
- Collaboration depends on shared responsibility for participation and decision making.
- Collaboration depends on individuals who share resources. Teachers in inclusive classrooms share resources such as skills, knowledge, and time.
- Individuals who collaborate share accountability for outcomes, whether they are positive or negative.

Coteaching

In the general education classroom, services for students with disabilities are often delivered through coteaching instructional models. Coteaching is "an educational approach in which general and special educators work in a coactive coordinated fashion to jointly teach academically and behaviorally heterogeneous groups of students in educationally integrated settings" (Bauwens, Hourcade, & Friend, 1989, p. 18).

Friend and Cook (2007) described six coteaching style approaches that teachers can implement in the inclusive classroom. No one style is preferred over another. When selecting an approach, coteachers should consider student needs, demands of the curriculum, and composition of the classroom.

The first coteaching style is *one teaching, one observing*. In this style, one teacher is responsible for designing and delivering instruction while the other teacher has the duty of collecting data on a single student, entire class, or a small group of students. It is an effective model, but if educators are not careful, it can result in one professional (typically the special educator) being relegated to that of an assistant. For this model to be effective, the educators should exchange roles regularly (Friend & Cook, 2007).

The second coteaching style is *station teaching*. In station teaching, students move from one station (i.e., center) to another according to a predetermined schedule. This approach actively involves both educators in instruction and allows both of them to take responsibility for planning and teaching. To be effective, coteachers prepare in advance and design lessons together (Friend & Cook, 2007). Special educators who teach in inclusive settings should be included in grade-level meetings relevant to their coteaching assignment so that adequate planning occurs (Pugach & Winn, 2011). Moreover, approaching coteaching with well-planned lessons ensures that interactions between the coteachers are satisfying as well as successful (Ploessl et al., 2010).

The third style of coteaching is *parallel teaching*. The primary purpose of parallel teaching is reducing the teacher-student ratio. In this type of coteaching, the teachers split the class in half and deliver the lesson to a smaller heterogeneous group of students. Parallel teaching requires that each teacher coordinate their lessons so that all students receive the same instruction. Moreover, the grouping decisions are based on maintaining diversity within each group. Specifically, students with disabilities are not all relegated to the group that is taught by the special educator (Friend & Cook, 2007).

Alternative teaching is the fourth style of coteaching. In this style, a small group of students receive specialized instruction from one of the teachers. This instruction is beneficial for highly intensive instruction in the general education classroom. However, one of the drawbacks of alternative teaching is that students with disabilities or those who are struggling may become stigmatized by repeatedly being pulled into the small group (Friend & Cook, 2007).

The fifth style of coteaching is *team teaching*, or *teaming*. In team teaching, both teachers share equally in planning and in the instruction of all students. Teaming requires that coteachers interweave their teaching styles and requires the greatest level of trust and commitment (Friend & Cook, 2007).

The final style of coteaching is *one teaching, one assisting*. In this style, one teacher primarily maintains control of the classroom while the second teacher assists students who need redirection or who have questions. One teaching, one assisting is the most widely used coteaching model, but it is the least effective and should only be used occasionally (Friend & Cook, 2007). In one teaching, one assisting, the special education teacher generally takes the backseat and acts as an assistant. If this occurs frequently, there is a potential that students will not perceive the special education teacher as a "real" teacher. If overused, this style can negatively impact the dynamics, interactions, and composition of the classroom.

Coteaching offers educators an opportunity to meet the needs of all learners in inclusive environments. However, for coteaching to be effective, educators must communicate with one another, engage in collaborative lesson planning, and practice effective conflict resolution. In particular, the educators involved must share a commitment to the coteaching process (Ploessl et al., 2010). In addition, both teachers should be committed to the process and involved in the discussions and planning before implementing any of the coteaching models.

TEACHER ROLES IN THE INCLUSIVE CLASSROOM

Even though teachers may possess positive dispositions toward including students with disabilities in general education environments and the ability to collaborate with one another, each professional has a distinct role to play in providing services in the inclusive classroom. It is vital that the educators teaching in inclusive environments remain open and flexible within their respective roles in order to provide services to students with disabilities.

General Education Teachers

General educators play a central role in providing educational services to students with disabilities in the inclusive classroom. In particular, they are expected to have knowledge of the curriculum and the curriculum standards that students are to learn and have the ability to design and implement instruction and activities so that every student can benefit from the instructional process (McLeskey et al., 2013). However, they may need to adapt particular aspects of the lesson, activity, or assignment, and they may need to become more educated about students with disabilities so that their planning is effective.

Special Education Teachers

When working with students with disabilities in the inclusive classroom, special education teachers should provide high-quality direct, intensive, and explicit instruction. McLeskey and Waldron (2011) argued that the role of the special education teacher in the inclusive environment should be limited to providing high-quality instruction for a finite period of time to small groups of students in one of the basic skill areas (i.e., reading, writing, or math). They also note that special education teachers should support general education teachers to ensure that high-quality instruction is provided in inclusive classroom settings.

Special educators may also provide indirect and supportive instruction. Examples of indirect instruction include conducting observations in the general education classroom and working with the general education teacher as a consultant in planning and designing high-quality lessons (McLeskey et al., 2013). These observations can provide invaluable information to aid the planning process.

Related Service Professionals

The Individuals with Disabilities Education Act (2004) requires related services for students with disabilities that are necessary to help them benefit from other educational services. Students may need additional therapies or services to help them in the areas of language or mobility to help them be successful. These services should always be considered when developing an IEP program. Examples of related service include physical therapy, occupational therapy, musical therapy, and counseling.

Related service personnel work very closely with the general education and special education teachers to support students who have services related to their disability. For example, a speech-language therapist may provide assistive technology equipment and services that enable a student with limited speech and language skills to communicate more effectively in the inclusive classroom. Related service personnel may also provide services, such as speech therapy, outside of the classroom in a separate setting. If this is the case, it would be important for the inclusion classroom teacher to communicate with the speech therapist to see if there is anything he or she could do to provide support in the classroom.

Occupational therapists and physical therapists also provide invaluable services to students with disabilities. These services may be provided in the inclusion classroom or as a pull-out service in a specialized setting. Occupational therapists, physical therapists, general education teachers, and special education teachers must work collaboratively when coordinating schedules so that students who need these services do not miss key instruction in the classroom. Therefore, it is critical that everyone works together in helping the student reach his or her individual education program goals in the least restrictive environment possible.

Paraeducators

Paraeducators perform a variety of supportive roles in the inclusive classroom. These activities may include tutoring a student after primary instruction has been given, reading a story aloud, and preparing materials and instructional activities and games (Correa, Jones, Thomas, & Morsink, 2005). Paraeducators who work in inclusive environments have the opportunity to positively impact the learning environment and to help students with disabilities adapt to the general education classroom (McLeskey et al., 2013).

ACCOMMODATIONS AND MODIFICATIONS

One of the challenges that teachers face in the inclusive classroom is how to effectively adapt or modify activities, assignments, and materials to meet the needs of students. Specifically, accommodations are alterations to curriculum, environment, instruction, and/or materials to meet the needs of students with disabilities in the general education classroom. Accommodations allow the student to achieve and demonstrate the same learning standards as others in the classroom (that is, accommodations cannot change the standard that the student is to achieve; McLeskey et al., 2013). For example, if the standard requires that the student write a one-paragraph summary containing four to five sentences, the teacher cannot change the standard to a one-paragraph summary with two to three sentences. However, an appropriate accommodation may involve the student using a computer or portable keyboarding device in writing the summary.

In other cases, it is unreasonable to expect that all students with disabilities will master the same general education curriculum objectives as their typically developing peers, even when accommodations and supplemental instruction are provided. In this case, modifications to the learning standard may be appropriate (McLeskey et al., 2013). Modifications change the learning standard and require a different method or degree of performance but are still based on general education grade-level standards (Westling & Fox, 2009).

The student's IEP will note the accommodations or modifications that are necessary. Examples of accommodations include highlighted text, recorded texts, manipulatives, assignment notebooks, repeated directions, calculator, and peer buddies. Table 4 provides examples of classroom accommodations for children with special needs.

Many children in the inclusive classroom may be served under IDEA (with an IEP) while others are served under a 504 Plan. Some examples of accommodations for 504 Plans or IEPs are included in the following table (see Table 5).

CONCLUSION

Belonging to a community of learners is a central construct for including students with disabilities in the general education environment. For inclusion to be effective, it is vital that the educators who work in inclusive classrooms remain positive toward inclusive practices. It necessitates a commitment to collaborate with one another, plan lessons together, and communicate on an ongoing basis with each other. When teachers engage in effective inclusive practices, it enables students with disabilities and their families to actively participate in the instructional process.

Table 4

EXAMPLES OF CLASSROOM ACCOMMODATIONS/MODIFICATIONS FOR CHILDREN WITH SPECIAL NEEDS

Disability	Classroom Environment	Curriculum Content	Instruction/Evaluation
Autism Spectrum Disorder	• Organize seating arrangements and classroom furniture to meet the needs of all children (maintain the structure of the physical environment as well as instructional environment) • Seat the child near the teacher or peer buddy as necessary (to support the use of peer tutoring) • Include quiet areas in classroom design • Use carpet squares to designate where the child should sit • The natural environment should support social interaction • Evaluate classroom lighting to determine its effect on child • Create a safe environment that offers protection from teasing and bullying	• Plan individual instruction for content knowledge • Review and determine the most appropriate curriculum for the child's needs • Be prepared to provide follow-up instruction • Provide a consistent classroom schedule and structure • Use simple instructions during lessons • Accept children's responses to questions • Enhance curriculum with the inclusion of social stories	• Encourage and reinforce positive behavior as it is exhibited • Monitor instruction and ask for feedback during lessons • Show a sample of the work that is expected from the child • Provide extended "wait time" for responses from the child • Provide self-monitoring checklists (with pictures or photographs) • Provide additional time for the child to complete his or her work • Use concrete objects as much as possible during instruction and evaluation • Evaluate use of instructional technology based on the individual needs of the child
Attention Deficit/ Hyperactivity Disorder (ADHD)	• Organize seating arrangements and classroom furniture to meet the needs of all children • Provide a highly structured environment (e.g., reduce wide open spaces) • Seat the child near the teacher or peer buddy as necessary • Provide soft background music	• Plan individual instruction for content knowledge • Be prepared to provide follow-up instruction • Consider classwide peer tutoring to support curriculum • Medication usage should be considered in curriculum and instructional planning • Avoid changes in routines and structures without offering a warning • Incorporate behavioral interventions including positive reinforcement	• Encourage and reinforce positive behavior as it is exhibited • Use concrete objects as much as possible during instruction and evaluation • Teach self-monitoring strategies
Speech and Language Impairments	• Organize seating arrangements and classroom furniture to meet the needs of all children • Seat the child near the teacher or peer buddy as necessary • Verbal participation should be promoted through the classroom design • Provide a language-rich environment	• Plan individual instruction for content knowledge • Instructional content should include social communication skills • Be prepared to provide follow-up instruction • Focus curriculum on both language comprehension and language expression (e.g., receptive and expressive language skills) • Incorporate technology that enhances and supports fluency	• Encourage and reinforce positive behavior as it is exhibited • Provide extended "wait time" for responses from child • Allow many opportunities for the child to use language • Use concrete objects as much as possible during instruction and evaluation • Model appropriate vocalizations throughout the child's daily instruction

Table 4, continued

Disability	Classroom Environment	Curriculum Content	Instruction/Evaluation
Hearing Impairments	◆ Organize seating arrangements and classroom furniture to meet the needs of all children ◆ Seat the child near the teacher or peer buddy as necessary (this holds especially true if the child is relying on residual hearing) ◆ When planning the environment take into consideration the external stimuli that might impact a child's use of specific technologies such as hearing aids or cochlear implants	◆ Plan individual instruction for content knowledge ◆ Be prepared to provide follow-up instruction ◆ Consider the need for interpreters when designing instructional content ◆ Plan for instruction using more frequent visual materials ◆ Plan group work with the individual student's needs taken into account	◆ Encourage and reinforce positive behavior as it is exhibited ◆ Avoid turning your back to the child when speaking to him or her ◆ Embed the use of graphic organizers to assist with instructional organization ◆ Integrate sign language with children throughout the day
Vision Impairments	◆ Organize seating arrangements and classroom furniture to meet the needs of all children; clear pathways as necessary ◆ Seat the child near the teacher or peer buddy as necessary ◆ Evaluate classroom lighting (e.g., brightness and contrast) to determine its effect on the child ◆ Evaluate the size of images and the student's needs when planning the environment	◆ Plan individual instruction for content knowledge ◆ Be prepared to provide follow-up instruction ◆ Incorporate orientation and mobility skills into curriculum ◆ Design instruction to include auditory models and hands-on manipulatives	◆ Encourage and reinforce positive behavior as it is exhibited ◆ Provide an introduction and sequence of events prior to instruction ◆ Instruction and evaluation can be optimized through the use of optical devices or Braille access software ◆ Locate and use books with large print during group presentations ◆ Provide instruction considering perceptual issues ◆ Use concrete objects and sensory materials as much as possible during instruction and evaluation
Orthopedic Impairments	◆ Organize seating arrangements and classroom furniture to meet the needs of all children; check for accessibility ◆ Design the environment to overcome architectural barriers ◆ Seat the child near the teacher or peer buddy for additional assistance as needed ◆ Evaluate the environment and make adjustments to furniture, writing utensils, coat racks, and art materials ◆ Lower or secure furniture as necessary ◆ Evaluate the portability of the materials within the environment	◆ Plan individual instruction for content knowledge ◆ Be prepared to provide follow-up instruction ◆ If deemed necessary, develop a healthcare plan that is individualized to meet the student's needs	◆ Encourage and reinforce positive behavior as it is exhibited ◆ Provide assistive technology devices, bookstands, or switches to facilitate instruction and evaluation ◆ Use concrete objects as much as possible during instruction and evaluation

Table 4, continued

Disability	Classroom Environment	Curriculum Content	Instruction/Evaluation
Intellectual Disabilities	◆ Organize seating arrangements and classroom furniture to meet the needs of all children ◆ Seat the child near the teacher or peer buddy as necessary ◆ Provide soft background music ◆ Be prepared to support the child's activity or assign a peer buddy ◆ Evaluate the environment and make adjustments to furniture, writing utensils, coat racks, and art materials	◆ Plan individual instruction for content knowledge ◆ Be prepared to provide follow-up instruction ◆ Provide consistent classroom schedule and structure that engages all students ◆ Use concrete objects when conducting mathematics activities ◆ Simplify complexity of expected tasks through task analysis ◆ Offer choices for activities that are limited in number	◆ Encourage and reinforce positive behavior as it is exhibited ◆ Provide more repetition and examples ◆ Use simple instructions during lessons ◆ Monitor instruction and ask for feedback during lessons ◆ Show a sample of the work that is expected from the child ◆ Provide extended "wait time" for responses from the child ◆ Provide time for the child to complete his or her work ◆ Use concrete objects as much as possible during instruction and evaluation
Traumatic Brain Injury (TBI)	◆ Organize seating arrangements and classroom furniture to meet the needs of all children (the environment should encourage mobility) ◆ Seat the child near the teacher or peer buddy as necessary ◆ Provide soft background music	◆ Plan individual instruction for content knowledge, taking into account that the learning and curriculum needs of students with TBI are continuously changing ◆ Be prepared to provide follow-up instruction ◆ If deemed necessary, develop a healthcare plan that is individualized to meet the student's needs	◆ Encourage and reinforce positive behavior as it is exhibited ◆ Use concrete objects as much as possible during instruction and evaluation
Learning Disabilities	◆ Organize seating to reduce distractions ◆ Follow a consistent routine or schedule ◆ Set, post, and explain classroom rules ◆ Use alternative books or materials on topics being studied ◆ Limit distractions and clutter in the classroom	◆ Use varied learning experiences (e.g., small-group instruction) ◆ Read or paraphrase subject matter ◆ Use peer tutoring or mentoring ◆ Review new content learned daily ◆ Limit, if possible, difficult vocabulary or paraphrase often	◆ Incorporate graphic organizers ◆ Provide shortened assignments ◆ Allow for untimed exams ◆ Use alternate ways to evaluate learning ◆ Read directions and tests to students

Note. Adapted from *Successful Inclusion Strategies for Early Childhood Teachers* (pp. 26–29) by C. G. Simpson and L. Warner, 2010, Waco, TX: Prufrock Press. Copyright 2010 Prufrock Press. Adapted with permission.

Table 5

EXAMPLES OF ACCOMMODATIONS AND MODIFICATIONS GIVEN TO STUDENTS WITH IEPS

Accommodations	• Large print • A reader • Books on tape • Screen reader (such as Kurzweil) • Notes, outlines, and instructions • Use of a scribe (someone writing down what you say) • Use of a word processor • Speech-to-text software programs • Respond directly in the test booklet • Use of a calculator • Use of a spell checking device • Use of graphic organizers • Extended time for tasks and assessments • Multiple or frequent breaks • Reduce distractions
Modifications	• Reduce written workload • Provide you with alternative ways to demonstrate mastery • Reduce the number of problems on a test or quiz
Supplemental Aids and Services	• Break long-term assignments down into smaller, more manageable pieces with interim due dates • Preferential seating • Use of a pencil grip • Checking your agenda book daily • Use of a carrel for independent work • Use of a specific reading program

Note. Adapted from *Take Control of Dyslexia and Other Reading Difficulties: The Ultimate Guide for Kids* (p. 10) by J. E. Fisher and J. Price, 2012, Waco, TX: Prufrock Press. Copyright 2012 Prufrock Press. Adapted with permission.

IF YOU WANT TO KNOW MORE

LD OnLine—http://www.ldonline.org
National Center for Learning Disabilities—http://www.ncld.org
National Center on Universal Design for Learning at CAST—http://www.udlcenter.org
Office of Special Education Programs—http://www.osepideasthatwork.org

CHAPTER 3

Doug

A STUDENT WITH AUTISM SPECTRUM DISORDER

Doug is a 10-year-old student with autism spectrum disorder enrolled in a public elementary school. His parents are concerned about Doug's eventual transition from the small elementary school to the much larger middle school.

Doug has been receiving services in a self-contained environment. However, when he is included, it is in the third grade general education setting. He attends physical education (P.E.) and art with the assistance of a paraprofessional. At a recent IEP meeting that spanned 3 days in which placement was the main concern, the committee finally agreed that Doug will begin to transition from the self-contained environment to a least restrictive setting in the attempt to get Doug ready for middle school. In addition to P.E. and art, Doug will now be included in third-grade social studies and science. Mrs. Zimmer, a certified special educator, will coteach the general education social studies and science classes. In addition, a Board Certified Behavior Specialist is providing consultation services to Doug's teachers and is working directly with Doug on a weekly basis.

Doug reads on the second-grade level and functions at the third-grade level in math. He likes playing games on the computer, surfing the Internet, and watching movies.

OVERVIEW OF AUTISM SPECTRUM DISORDERS

What Are Autism Spectrum Disorders?

Autism is a group of developmental brain disorders, collectively called autism spectrum disorders (ASD). Different students with autism can have very different symptoms and exhibit very different behaviors. The term *spectrum* refers to the wide range of symptoms, skills, and levels of impairment, or disability, that children with ASD can have. Like other disabilities, one person may have mild symptoms, while another may have serious symptoms, but they still both have ASD. The category of autism spectrum disorders includes Asperger's syndrome, autism, and Pervasive Developmental Disorder–Not Otherwise Specified (PDD–NOS).

Symptoms of ASD usually start before age 3 and can cause delays or problems in many different skills that develop from infancy to adulthood. Autism is characterized by a developmental disability significantly affecting a child's social interaction and verbal and nonverbal communication and adversely affecting learning and educational performance. Other characteristics often associated with autism are resistance to environmental change or change in daily routines, engagement in repetitive activities and stereotyped movements, and unusual responses to sensory experiences.

What Teachers Need to Know About Autism Spectrum Disorders

Students with autism spectrum disorders typically display difficulties in interactions with people and events. Establishing and maintaining reciprocal relationships with people could be very difficult for them. A teacher who establishes consistent routines and follows a specific schedule will help students with ASD. In addition, when changes do occur, the teacher should notify students with ASD (and parents) to prepare them for the change. Another issue could be with communication and how these students interact with the teacher and/or other students. Students with ASD could have both receptive and expressive language difficulties, as well as speech and/or language disorders. If this is the case, the teacher should be aware of how a particular student with autism typically communicates. Students with ASD could also exhibit various delays, or have difficulties with social, sensory, or learning skills. Some skills may be deficient while other skills may be advanced. The teacher should be aware of a student's strengths and weaknesses. With regard to thinking, the teacher may find that anything abstract is difficult for a student with autism, while he or she has an easier time grasping more concrete thinking. Last, students with ASD may also be sensitive to touch, sound, smells, or movement. To learn about individual students, communication with other teachers and parents are essential.

INCLUSIVE CLASSROOM STRATEGIES

Family Interventions

Families with children with ASD often need long-term support services. Children with autism demonstrate characteristics throughout their lifespan with some individuals requiring supervision even as adults. Children with ASD benefit from a team approach among families, related service providers, classroom teachers, and caregivers.

When trying to treat the symptoms of autism, the individual's family must be involved and must buy into the interventions that are proposed. They know their child best and can assist in recommending interventions that will be the most effective. They are valuable resources to the interventionists by giving information about the behaviors of the student. In some cases, the family will need to use some of the intervention strategies at home for consistency.

Classroom Interventions

Teachers who work with children with autism must have specific training in ASD. They should also participate in ongoing professional development workshops to further their knowledge and skills when working with children who have ASD. They should be aware of key interventions that children with ASD may need in order to achieve success in the classroom environment. Some of the key interventions are:
- consistent routine/schedule,
- Applied Behavior Analysis,
- modeling,
- Social Stories, and
- communication.

Consistent routine/schedule. Predictable and consistent environments are critical for children who have ASD. Children with ASD typically have difficulty with transitioning from activity to activity, and they need a consistent schedule that is easy to understand and follow. Daily schedules that are paired with pictures help children with ASD to anticipate the day's activities and prepare for the demands that are expected of them. Figure 6 shows a daily picture schedule developed for an elementary school setting.

Applied Behavior Analysis. Applied behavior analysis (ABA) is based on the principle that behaviors can be changed by modifying the child's environment. Applied behavior analysis focuses on studying the behavior and finding the function of the behavior. Individuals who are Board Certified Behavior Analysts (BCBA) have specific training and skills in applying ABA techniques. By completing a functional behavior analysis, the antecedent (the event that occurs before the behavior), the target behavior, and the consequences are identified. By observing the antecedents, the behavior, and the consequence, the interventionists (i.e., BCBA, teacher) are able to determine what is causing the behavior and what is reinforcing the behavior. After the function of the behavior is determined, a behavior intervention plan is developed to decrease inappropriate behavior and increase desired behaviors. The steps and processes involved with applied behavior analysis aid in finding an intervention that will be most effective in treating problem behaviors.

Using reinforcements while trying to modify behaviors is an effective method for decreasing problem behaviors. There are many different types of reinforcement, including edible reinforcement (e.g., food), physical reinforcement (e.g., high five or a hug), and tangible reinforcement (e.g., token systems or stickers). There are different ways to use reinforcement to modify behavior. Reinforcement can be used as a punishment to diminish inappropriate behaviors. When an inappropriate target behavior occurs, a negative reinforcement can be used to deter the behavior from happening again. Reinforcement can also be used as a reward to increase appropriate behaviors. When a desired behavior occurs, the reinforcement is given as a prize or a reward to increase the occurrence. Differential reinforcement of alternate behavior involves withholding reinforcement when an undesired behavior occurs and then giving the reinforcement when a desired behavior occurs. Extinction is taking away the reinforcement of a previously reinforced behavior.

During the functional behavior assessment, the reinforcement of the behavior is identified. For example, if a child is misbehaving and exhibiting off task behaviors such as making unwanted noises, and, as a consequence, the teacher takes the child's work away, the child is being rewarded by escaping the academic task. The teacher wants the student to complete the work, so taking it away is not what the teacher should do. Instead, the teacher may want to reward the student for behaving appropriately and completing her work. The teacher may speak with the student and/or the parent and find out what might be appropriate reinforcements to implement when this type of behavior occurs. For example, maybe the student likes to work on the computer. Upon completion of their homework with at least 80% accuracy, the student is provided with 10 minutes of computer time. This

Figure 6. Daily picture schedule. From *Successful Inclusion Strategies for Early Childhood Teachers* (p. 46) by C. G. Simpson and L. Warner, 2010, Waco, TX: Prufrock Press. Copyright 2010 Prufrock Press. Reprinted with permission.

type of reinforcement may prove very beneficial as the teacher gets what he or she wants (i.e., completed homework) and the student gets reinforced for completing the task and behaving appropriately.

Modeling. Another type of intervention used to decrease aggressive behaviors and increase desired behaviors in children with autism is modeling of desired behaviors. There are many different effective ways to model behaviors for children with autism. Modeling appropriate behaviors teaches children with ASD skills that they can use in everyday life, such as washing their hands after using the toilet, communicating with peers, and getting dressed in the mornings. Modeling gives children visual instructions on how to complete tasks and how to interact with peers.

Video modeling, a specific method of modeling, has emerged as an intervention for students with autism. Video models are visual interventions that use self, peers, or adults as models and that are individualized for the student. Videos are created for skills in a variety of areas (such as communication, social, or functional living) and in a wide array of settings (e.g. home, school, and community; Delano, 2007). Ganz, Vollrath, and Cook (2011) explained that "video modeling is a strategy involving the use of videos to provide modeling of targeted skills. Both videos that include the participant and videos of others have been found effective in teaching the skills" (p. 9).

Video modeling has been used effectively to improve different skills and target behaviors (such as social interaction behaviors, communication skills, perspective taking, and social initiations) and to reduce problem behaviors (Ganz et al., 2011). Moreover, video models are particularly suitable for students with autism who may have significant language deficits and find it challenging to attend to information being presented by the teacher or to engage in social interactions (Delano, 2007).

Social Stories. Another intervention that is similar to video modeling is social story intervention. Just like with video modeling, social stories are used to teach appropriate behaviors in social situations. One method of using social stories as an intervention involves reading the social story to the student regularly or having the student interact with the social story in collaboration with the teacher. Then the child is observed in social situations to see if the directives in the story are generalized. If not, additional interaction with the social story may be necessary. Spencer, Simpson, and Lynch (2008) explained that "social stories follow an explicit format of approximately 5–10 sentences describing the social skill, the appropriate behavior, and other's viewpoints of the actions" (p. 59). The following is a sample social story that depicts the appropriate sentence design (Spencer et al., 2008):

Recess Time

We like to play with toys during recess time. (descriptive sentence)

When it is time to clean up after recess time, my teacher sings the clean up song. (descriptive sentence)

Sometimes we are having fun playing and do not want to clean up. (descriptive sentence)

After we clean up our toys, we can go inside for snacks. (descriptive sentence)

Even when we want to keep playing, we pick up our toys. (directive sentence)

My teacher is happy when we pick up our toys. (perspective sentence)

It is important to keep our toys neat and to pick up. (perspective sentence)

I will remember to pick up my toys when I hear the clean up song at recess. (control sentence). (p. 60)

Communication. Children with ASD often lack communication skills. This lack of skills often precipitates problems in the classroom environment. Using a picture exchange system can help children with autism to communicate their wants and needs and reduce the risk of frustration. When a child cannot effectively communicate wants and needs, his or her frustration turns into disruptive and aggressive behaviors. Providing a child with ASD with a way to communicate enables him to receive what he wants and needs in order to achieve success.

APPLYING THE STRATEGIES

At a recent IEP meeting that spanned 3 days in which placement was the main concern, the committee finally agreed that Doug will begin to transition from the self-contained environment to a least restrictive setting in the attempt to get Doug ready for middle school. In addition to P.E. and art, Doug will now be included in third-grade social studies and science. Mrs. Zimmer, a certified special educator, will coteach the general education social studies and science classes.

Before transitioning Doug from the self-contained environment to a more inclusive environment, the team must plan in advance so that the transition occurs smoothly for Doug and for the other students in the social studies and science classrooms. Following are specific strategies that Mrs. Zimmer and the rest of the IEP team used to ensure a smooth transition.

Working With the Whole Class

When working with the whole class, Mrs. Zimmer and Mr. Roland incorporated the following strategies:

◻ *Communicate with the general education teacher.* Before transitioning Doug to the general education setting for social studies and science, Mrs. Zimmer met with Mr. Roland and reviewed the contents of Doug's IEP, even though Mr. Roland had been present at the meeting. During this meeting, they discussed accommodations, grading practices, and how to specifically implement Doug's goals and objectives in Mr. Roland's classroom. This meeting allowed Mr. Roland to specifically address any concerns he had and to brainstorm possible solutions. Prior to Doug's first day in class, Mr. Roland explained to his students that they would be receiving a new classmate, Doug, in a few days, and that Doug would require specific strategies and would have needs that may be different from other students in the classroom. During this classwide discussion, Mr. Roland identified prospective peer buddies for Doug.

◻ *Post a daily schedule.* Although Mr. Roland posted the daily schedule and reviewed it periodically with his students, he made the schedule more prominent and, with the assistance of Mrs. Zimmer, paired pictures with the schedule.

◻ *Communicate with families.* Mr. Roland and Mrs. Zimmer wrote in Doug's communication folder every day. In this folder, they noted the class lessons/activities, goals for Doug for the lessons, behaviors that may have occurred, and progress toward goals and objectives. By using a communication log that went home daily in Doug's backpack, Doug's parents were informed as to the happenings of the class and Doug's behavior and progress.

Working With Individual Children

When working with Doug, Mrs. Zimmer and Mr. Roland incorporated the following strategies:

◻ *Assign peer buddies.* Mr. Roland assigned peer buddies to Doug before his first day in the classroom. By working with the peer buddies in advance of Doug's arrival, the buddies were better able to understand how they might assist Doug during transitions, cooperative group time, and during other times that he might need support.

- *Use a picture exchange system.* Mrs. Zimmer continued to use the picture exchange system that she had been using in the self-contained environment in Mr. Roland's social studies and science classroom. Mrs. Zimmer taught Mr. Roland and Doug's classmates how Doug used the picture exchange system to communicate his wants and needs.

- *Facilitate social interactions.* Mr. Roland was able to facilitate social interactions by assigning Doug peer buddies to help improve his relationships with his peers in a nonthreatening environment. In addition, the peer buddies were trained in using the picture exchange system that Doug used so he could communicate with his buddies. Doug learned how to ask his buddies simple questions, and they were able to respond to him in return.

- *Post a visual schedule.* Mr. Roland posted a picture schedule at the top of Doug's desk. Along with Mrs. Zimmer, Doug's peer buddies were able to help Doug prepare for transitions and the activities in the class.

- *Use video modeling.* Mrs. Zimmer and Mr. Roland worked with Doug's family and peers to develop video models to help Doug with social interactions in the classroom and on the playground. These videos presented Doug with a variety of prosocial models and opportunities to develop social skills in a safe environment.

- *Provide individualized reinforcement.* Because Doug was already working with a BCBA, an individualized behavior intervention plan (BIP) and a reinforcement schedule had been developed and updated at the IEP meeting. Mr. Roland and Mrs. Zimmer worked with the BCBA in implementing the BIP in Mr. Roland's classroom. Mr. Roland continued to use classwide reinforcements strategies but knew that Doug preferred certain reinforcers and activities. For example, one of Doug's preferred activities was playing computer games. When Doug successfully participated in an activity, he was given the opportunity to have 5 minutes playing a computer game of his choice.

Working With Families

Involving families of children who have ASD is a critical component of the child's overall success in the school and home environment. Specific strategies that families could use in the home environment are:

- *Maintain a consistent schedule.* Just as in the school environment, a consistent schedule is critical for a smooth home life for a family who has a child with ASD. Providing a picture schedule for everyday routines, such as getting ready, eating, and bedtime, helps to ensure that the child with ASD completes each activity with little conflict.

- *Maintain an organized environment.* Families can assist their child with ASD in providing an organized environment. Visual boundaries for toys (such as a rug) could be used for playing with certain toys, puzzles, etc. Further, children should be taught to put things away where they belong. Provide bins and crates for toys that the child plays with and model putting the toys away when they are finished playing.
- *Keep directions short.* Parents should limit directions for tasks to one and two steps. Pairing directions with picture cues will help the child understand what she or he is supposed to do.
- *Work with related service providers.* Children with ASD often have related service personnel such as in-home training and parent training. Working with the professionals who provide in-home training and parent training can benefit the entire family unit and help to enhance the family's overall quality of life.

IF YOU WANT TO KNOW MORE

Autism Speaks—http://www.autismspeaks.org
Foundation for Autistic Childhood Education and Support—http://facesforkids.org
Child-Autism-Parent-Café.com: Teaching Autism Students in Inclusive Classroom—http://www.child-autism-parent-cafe.com/autism-students-in-inclusive-classrooms.html
The Division of Autism and Developmental Disabilities—http://daddcec.org/Home.aspx

4

Jared

A STUDENT WITH ATTENTION DEFICIT/ HYPERACTIVITY DISORDER

Jared is a 10-year-old child who has recently been diagnosed with Attention Deficit/Hyperactivity Disorder (ADHD). He lives with his biological mother, sister, and stepfather. Jared's biological parents have differing parenting styles. His mother maintains a consistent and stable home life, while his father's home is typically unstructured and less consistent. Jared is consistently on medication while he is at his mother's home and sporadically when he is visiting his father.

Jared mostly obtains A's and B's in school but has difficulty with accepting responsibility for his behavior. His teacher, Mrs. Moreno, reports that Jared has difficulty with attention to task, organization, and submitting his homework without verbal reminders. Because Jared's grades are good, Jared's father doesn't understand why Jared cannot control his actions and acts so impulsively. Ms. Moreno is struggling to address the challenging behaviors that Jared exhibits at school and feels that the disconnect between parenting styles is to blame for the difficulties that Jared is exhibiting.

OVERVIEW OF ATTENTION DEFICIT/ HYPERACTIVITY DISORDER (ADHD)

What Is ADHD?

ADHD is one of the most common childhood disorders. It can be found in elementary-aged students and continues through adolescence and adulthood. Symptoms of this disorder include difficulty controlling behavior, difficulty staying focused and paying attention, and hyperactivity (overactivity). ADHD is comprised of three different subtypes: predominantly hyperactive-impulsive, predominately inattentive, and a combined hyperactive-impulsive and inattentive.

With each of these are associated characteristics. For the predominantly hyperactive-impulsive category, most symptoms (six or more) are in the hyperactivity-impulsivity categories used to diagnose the disorder. Fewer than six symptoms of inattention are present, although inattention may still be present to some degree. Some example behaviors include difficulty remaining seated, difficulty quietly engaging in activities, talking excessively, blurting out answers before questions are finished being asked, and difficulty with taking turns.

For the predominately inattentive category, the majority of symptoms (six or more) are in the inattention category used to diagnose the disorder, and fewer than six symptoms of hyperactivity-impulsivity are present, although hyperactivity-impulsivity may still be present to some degree. Some example inattentive behaviors include difficulty sustaining attention, difficulty with organization, often loses things, does not appear to listen, and avoids or dislikes mental effort. Children with this subtype are less likely to act out or have difficulties getting along with other children. They may sit quietly, but they are not paying attention to what they are doing. Therefore, the child may be overlooked, and parents and teachers may not notice that he or she has ADHD. Finally, for the combined hyperactive-impulsive and inattentive category, the student meets the criteria for both hyperactivity-impulsivity and inattentiveness. There are treatments that are effective in relieving many of ADHD's symptoms, but there is no cure.

What Teachers Need to Know About Attention Deficit Hyperactivity Disorder

For teachers, it is normal to come across children who are inattentive, hyperactive, or impulsive. Most students exhibit some episodes of these types of behaviors, but they aren't excessive. For students with ADHD, however, these behaviors are more severe and occur more often. To be diagnosed with ADHD, the student must exhibit symptoms for 6 or more months and to a degree that is greater than other children their same age. ADHD can impact the learning of a student in a classroom. In addition, the learning of other students around him could be altered as well. It is important that teachers are very aware if there are patterns of student behavior that might impact his learning or the learning of others.

Things that teachers can look for include students who are easily distracted, miss details, forget things, and frequently switch from one activity to another. They might have a difficult time focusing on a task or easily become bored after only a few minutes working on the task. They could also have difficulty with attention, organization, completing a task, trouble completing or turning in homework assignments, losing things (e.g., pencils, toys, assignments), and not listening. Other characteristics include daydreaming, fidgeting in their seats, non-stop talking, or being constantly in motion. Again, if a student exhibits a few of these behaviors once in a while, there is probably not a problem. If the student exhibits many of these behaviors persistently, then the teacher should be in communication with the parent about what is happening.

It is important for inclusive classroom teachers to understand that students with ADHD may be taking some type of medication to help them stay more focused during school. The most widely used medications tend to be amphetamine stimulants (i.e., Adderall, Dexedrine, and Adderall XR), methylphenidate stimulants (i.e., Methylin, Ritalin, and Concerta), and antidepressants (i.e., Wellbutrin, Tofranol, and Aventyl). The inclusive classroom teacher, along with the school nurse, should monitor the student with ADHD who is taking medication, especially if the medication being implemented is new. Is the medication effective? Is the medication helping the student? Does the student fall asleep? Are there any side effects of taking the medication apparent in school? The inclusive classroom teacher should probably communicate daily with the parents, providing information on academics and behavior as a result of the medication. Because every student is different and may experience different ADHD symptoms, each medication may have a different impact on an individual student as well. It may take multiple trials before the most appropriate medication for the student with ADHD is found, so communication between the inclusive classroom teacher and parents is critical. Davis et al. (2011) suggested the following tips for parents considering medication for their children with ADHD:

- Seek the best help for medication consultation! Ask your pediatrician, therapist, family, and friends for names of physicians. Make sure to check their credentials.
- Do not be afraid to ask questions. The physician must be able to explain what he or she is recommending to your satisfaction. If you are not sure whether to ask a question, ask anyway.
- Learn as much as you can about the medication.
- There is no magic cure. Medication can help but it must be used in combination with other nonmedication interventions.

◻   If the medication is not working, reevaluate or get a second opinion. The diagnosis may be correct but there can be another coexisting condition that is not being addressed. Children are constantly developing and their diagnosis is always evolving or changing.

◻   Always consider nonmedication options along with medications. Lifestyle and daily routines such as sleeping patterns, nutrition, and activities can improve or worsen symptoms.

◻   Review your family history for psychiatric disorders and medication response of relatives. Most psychiatric disorders such as ADHD, anxiety, and depression have a genetic or familial predisposition. This information will help your physician with considerations for diagnosis and treatment.

◻   Do not change your child's medication without the physician's consent. Some medications can have dangerous effects if stopped abruptly or when doses are changed.

◻   Use daily logs to monitor changes you observe in your child while on medication. Changes in mood, behavior, weight, appetite, sleep, energy, and school performance are hard to recall when you see the physician. It is important to bring this information at every physician visit. This will help guide medication adjustment.

◻   Are brand medications better than generic? There is no simple answer as it can vary from one medication to another. Generic drugs cost less but not all drugs are available in generic form. Newer drugs are not available as generics for several years. There are several companies that can make the generic drug, therefore the quality control can vary. The child might be sensitive to the inactive ingredient of the drug such as the coloring or dye and this can affect her reaction. (pp. 264–265)

Davis et al. (2011) also provided tips for teachers to remember when working with students with ADHD and medications:

1.   Do not suggest medications to parents.

2.   Be open and flexible to suggestions from parents and medical providers, as their goal is the same as yours. You all want the child to behave and perform to the best of his or her ability.

3.   Stimulant medications for ADHD work quickly, therefore there will be a major change in behavior and performance when the child has missed his or her daily dose.

4.   Medications for mood take 2–6 weeks to start working; however, the side effects can occur early. Sedation, agitation, and appetite changes can be caused by medications.

5.   Tell parents right away if you notice any significant change in mood, attention, alertness, orientation, and behavior, as these changes can be

signs of medication toxicity or due to a serious medical condition such as seizures.

6. Anger and defiance can mask depression and anxiety in school-aged children. Active listening and patience generally will work better than negative reinforcement and can help reduce tension in a volatile situation. Adolescents are highly sensitive to shame and embarrassment, especially in a school setting. It is extremely important to talk to them privately instead of in the presence of their peers.

7. Never compromise your safety and that of your students.

8. Call parents to share positive and negative feedback about their child. This will improve your credibility to both the child and the parents.

9. Refrain from making comments about the child's medication in class, as each child has a different sentiment about medication. The child could become the object of teasing or bullying once peers know he or she has a condition or takes medications.

10. Open communication is always best between the school and the family. Teachers have a very important role and influence in a child's life and, next to the parents, no one spends as much time with the child as teachers do. (pp. 265–266)

INCLUSIVE CLASSROOM STRATEGIES

Family Interventions

Families with children who have ADHD may experience more stress and a lower quality of life than families who have children who develop more typically (Lange et al., 2005). For example, "parents of youths diagnosed with ADHD in childhood were more likely to divorce by the time their children were 8 years of age (22.7%) than were parents of youths without ADHD (12.6%)" (Wymbs et al., 2008, p. 741). In addition, research suggests that attention disorders are genetically based and tend to run in families. Estimates suggest that as many as 32% of children with ADHD have parents or siblings with ADHD (Biederman et al., 1992).

Children who have ADHD exhibit disorders in executive functioning—the ability to plan, organize, control impulses, and complete tasks. Thus, it is imperative that parents assist their child who has ADHD with executive functioning behaviors as they acquire skills in coping with the demands of their environment (Smith & Segal, 2012).

Strategies that parents can implement within the home environment include maintaining a consistent and structured home environment and setting clear expectations and rules. Children with ADHD need to follow established, predictable routines for meals, play, waking, bed, and any other activities that the family engages in. Parents can also assist their child by setting clocks and timers for routine tasks (e.g., for homework, extracurricular activities, and getting ready in the mornings). Finally, parents of children with ADHD should demonstrate organization within the home environment. Emphasize that everything has its place and hold the child accountable for placing items where they belong. For example, dirty laundry is placed in the laundry basket in the laundry room and not the floor of his or her bedroom (Smith & Segal, 2012).

Classroom Interventions

Teachers of students with ADHD must have a good understanding of a wide variety of strategies, especially strategies that are related to executive functioning, such as organization, maintaining attention to task, and self-regulation. Moreover, teachers must set clear expectations and rules and implement behavioral interventions.

Executive functioning. A cognitive processing skill that is related to children with ADHD is executive functioning, which controls cognitive processing and manages all other types of processing. Generally, skills such as goal setting, planning, problem solving, self-monitoring, self-regulating, self-evaluating, and adjusting are characteristics of executive functions (Dehn, 2006). Research indicates that dysfunctions within executive functions become more apparent as children move through the early elementary grades. As the difficulty of academic tasks increases with grades, the demands of completing schoolwork independently can trigger signs of a problem with executive function (National Center for Learning Disabilities, 2010).

Teaching specific organization skills will help children with ADHD to approach tasks more efficiently and effectively. Provide an assignment book in which the child writes his homework for each class (or if writing is difficult, have a peer write the assignment in the notebook). The teacher needs to check it for legibility and accuracy and sign it. If there is no homework, indicate that there is no homework assigned. At home, the parent checks the assignment book and signs the assignment notebook for each completed assignment.

Students with ADHD often have assignments completed, but their papers are unorganized and/or they forget to turn in the completed work. Teachers can facilitate organization by providing a homework folder that the child may use to transport homework to and from school. One side of the folder should be labeled "homework to be completed," and the other side should be called "completed homework." As he or she completes each assignment, the child moves the assign-ment to the completed side of the folder. Once at school, teachers should remind the child to turn in his homework (e.g., with verbal cues or visual cues placed in her or his work area) to be sure that he turns in homework appropriately (Mather & Jaffe, 2002).

Self-regulation is the ability to monitor and self-manage one's behavior. It is also used to manage interactions within the learning environment (Singer & Bashir, 1999). Students must be able to self-regulate their behavior and learning in academic settings to experience success. Self-regulation and executive functions are vital to cognitive, linguistic, and behavioral control, all of which are primary for learning and academic success.

Self-management. The primary components of self-management are self-monitoring (i.e., self-observation, self-recording), self-evaluation, and self-re-inforcement (Shogren, Land, Machalicek, Rispoli, & O'Reilly, 2010). Self-management interventions may be used with students at any age level with any identifiable disability as well as with students suspected of having ADHD (King-Sears, 2006).

Self-management strategies take on many forms. Most of these strategies are created through collaborative efforts between teacher and student where both par-ties contribute to the development and implementation of the strategy. Frequently, the result of this collaboration will take on the form of a chart that can either be maintained in a folder located somewhere in the classroom or placed on the stu-dent's desk. Students are then assigned the responsibility of keeping up with the charts. A purpose for this strategy could be that the student will self-monitor his or her behavior and the teacher can immediately review and evaluate progress, or lack thereof, by simply walking past and glancing at the chart. These charts are used for on-task or desirable behavior, assignment completion, safety rules, and as a method for students to appropriately request assistance (see Figure 7).

The Focusing Together Program: A self-management strategy. The Focusing Together Program promotes self-management skills in the classroom. The first thing that students learn as they proceed through the steps of the strategy is how to live by a set of learning community expectations that help them interact positively with other members of the class and complete their work in a timely manner. Secondly, students learn how their choices of whether or not to abide by the class expectations impact their personal power. Finally, students learn a self-management strategy (the FOCUS Strategy) that will help them stay on task when asked to work independently or in small groups (Rademacher, Pemberton, & Cheever, 2006). The FOCUS Strategy is incorporated within the Focusing Together Program and serves as a memory tool for children to remember the specific steps of the strategy.

Follow the three rules:
- ◆ Write name on paper.
- ◆ Answer all questions in assignment.
- ◆ Turn assignment in.

Subject	🙂	✗
Writing		
Reading		
Math		
Science		

Today I am working for: _____

Student signature

Figure 7. Example of self-management chart for a child with ADHD.

In a research study conducted by Rademacher et al. (2006) to measure the effects of the Focusing Together Program on teacher and student behavior, students in the experimental group engaged in an average of five off-task behaviors as compared to the comparison group (those who did not receive The Focusing Together Program), who engaged in an average of 18 off-task behaviors in a 45-minute period. Prior to the beginning of the intervention, the experimental students and comparison students each engaged in an average of 21 and 22 off-task behaviors within a 45-minute period of time. The results of the study indicated that students reduced the number of off-task behaviors during independent work times, teachers were satisfied with the program and student's behavior, teachers reported reduction in off-task behaviors, and students were more pleased at the end of the study than at the beginning of the study.

The seven Focusing Together lessons help students understand how to manage their own behaviors in a supportive environment. During the lessons, students learn how to meet a set of expectations, how to make good choices in problem situations, and how to manage themselves as they work alone or with others (Rademacher et al., 2006). The following is a brief overview of each of the seven lessons as described in the manual.

     ◻   Lesson 1: Introduction and Overview. As part of this overview, the teacher guides students to quickly identify some expectations of an effective learning community.

     ◻   Lesson 2: Our Learning Community Expectations. At the beginning of this lesson, the teacher displays a list that summarizes the learning community expectations brainstormed in the first lesson.

     ◻   Lesson 3: Making Good Choices. Students participate in a discussion to learn about the relationship between the choices they make about meeting or not meeting expectations and the consequences—negative or positive—related to these choices.

- ☐ Lesson 4: Introduce and Describe the FOCUS Strategy. Here, students are introduced to the steps of the FOCUS Strategy. The FOCUS Strategy consists of 5 primary steps: (1) **F**ree your mind of distractions, (2) **O**rganize yourself, (3) **C**heck the expectations and get started, (4) **U**se help wisely, and (5) **S**upervise yourself.

- ☐ Lesson 5: Model the FOCUS Strategy. Students watch the teacher perform the FOCUS Strategy.

- ☐ Lesson 6: Verbal Practice of the FOCUS Strategy. Students practice saying the names of the steps of the FOCUS Strategy and their meanings.

- ☐ Lesson 7: Practice the FOCUS Strategy. Here, the teacher provides students with opportunities to practice the strategy and teaches them how to monitor their application of the strategy by completing the FOCUS Checklist. (Rademacher et al., 2006, pp. 5–6, 63)

Students who use self-management techniques, such as charting behaviors during a given period of time and employing the Focusing Together Program, improve the likelihood of academic success. Further, educators who teach specific self-management strategies are more likely to have increased student outcomes and overall satisfaction with the learning process.

APPLYING THE STRATEGIES

Jared has difficulty with accepting responsibility for his behavior. His teacher, Mrs. Moreno, reports that Jared has difficulty with attention to task, organization, and submitting his homework without verbal reminders.

Prior to the beginning of the school year, Mrs. Moreno attended a professional development workshop on children with ADHD and had insight into what kinds of behaviors Jared might exhibit in the classroom. Because she had some knowledge and skills in working with children who had ADHD, she was better able to ascertain which accommodations Jared would need in her classroom.

Working With the Whole Class

Following are some of the strategies that Mrs. Moreno used with her whole class:

- ☐ *State clear expectations and rules.* Mrs. Moreno posted the rules and provided a visual cue for each rule. She reviewed the expectations in her classroom on the first day of school. She also modeled and demonstrated the rules and expectations during the first week of school, providing positive reinforcement and corrective feedback when needed.

- *Post a schedule.* Mrs. Moreno posted a written and visual schedule of the activities for each day and the time that each activity occurs. She reviewed the schedule at the beginning of each day and provided advanced notice when transitions were about to occur.

- *Organize the classroom and maintain a routine.* Mrs. Moreno organized her classroom so that students began the day with specific procedures and proceeded through the day with clear routine and consistency. As she modeled the structure of the day, students were taught to turn in items in a specific location and how to transition from activity to activity with ease. Mrs. Moreno also implemented a homework folder and log for each student. Parents were to initial the homework log after their child completed each assignment and placed their homework in the folder.

Working With Individual Children

Following are some of the strategies that Mrs. Moreno used with Jared:

- *Use a self-management chart.* Because Jared had difficulty accepting responsibility for his behavior in class and maintaining attention to task, Mrs. Moreno decided to implement a simple behavior chart. Jared would earn smiley face stickers for each 5-minute period of time that he was engaged in on-task behavior during independent work time. At the end of the day, Jared would earn a trip to the treasure box if he reached his goal.

- *Provide acceptable alternatives.* Mrs. Moreno provided Jared with limited alternatives during center time. For example, she might say, "Jared you can go to the reading center or the math center. Which do you prefer?" She also planned carefully the activities and the choices that she made available to Jared so as not to overwhelm him and to promote decision making within specified parameters.

- *Provide cues.* Mrs. Moreno provided Jared with a visual schedule at his desk of when specific assignments were to be submitted. She also equipped Jared with a WatchMinder, a watch that signaled Jared to submit homework at certain times. As a training device, the WatchMinder may also be programmed to vibrate at regular intervals to signal Jared to do certain behaviors, such as ask himself if he is actively working. (WatchMinder is available from http://www.watchminder.com.)

- *Provide thoughtful classroom seating arrangements:* During independent work times, Jared was provided with a study carrel so that he could work without distractions from his neighbors. Mrs. Moreno also arranged the classroom so that Jared's seat was near her when she was giving whole-group lessons and during small-group instruction.

Working With Families

Following are some of the strategies that Mrs. Moreno used with Jared's family:

- *Meet face-to-face with parents.* Mrs. Moreno scheduled four meetings during the year to sit down with Jared's parents (mother, stepfather, and father) to discuss Jared's progress and any concerns they have. By providing frequent feedback via the assignment notebook and through these meetings, Jared's parents and Mrs. Moreno were better able to work together to help Jared achieve academic success.

- *Research and read.* Mrs. Moreno continued to read about ADHD and attended an additional professional development workshop to further her knowledge of children with ADHD. She also provided Jared's parents with a list of resources that they could investigate to help assist Jared in the home environment. (See "If You Want to Know More" at the end of the chapter to learn about some of the resources that Mrs. Moreno thought were helpful.)

- *Develop a behavior incentive plan.* Mrs. Moreno and Jared's parents developed a behavior incentive plan that rewarded Jared with his preferred activities when he achieved his goal on his self-management chart. By working together, Mrs. Moreno and Jared's parents were able to remain consistent with each other regarding their expectations of Jared's behavior in school.

IF YOU WANT TO KNOW MORE

ADHD Aware—http://www.adhdaware.org/understanding-adhd/resources

LD Online—http://www.ldonline.org/index.php

ADD/ADHD and School, Helping Children With ADHD Succeed at School— http://helpguide.org/mental/adhd_add_teaching_strategies.htm

Accommodations for ADHD Students—http://www.addcoach4u.com/teaching students/adhdaccomodations.html

ADHD Fact Sheet—http://www.athealth.com/consumer/disorders/nichcy_ adhd.html

5

Yojanna

A STUDENT WITH LEARNING DISABILITIES

Yojanna is a 9-year-old girl in the third grade. Her father and stepmother are concerned about her reading ability. Her biological mother and father are divorced and are in a custody battle over Yojanna and her brother. Yojanna currently lives in a rural area with her father and stepmother who have sole guardianship rights but share joint educational rights with Yojanna's biological mother. Her biological mother also has visitation rights.

Yojanna attends class in a general education classroom. Her teacher, Ms. Smyth, is also concerned about Yojanna's reading ability and has referred her to the student support team for a possible special education evaluation. Ms. Smyth conducts small-group instruction with Yojanna but has not seen measurable improvements in her reading ability. Yojanna has the reading ability of a second grader, with a reading fluency rate of 95 words correct per minute. Her reading skill is impacting her ability to be successful in other academic areas.

OVERVIEW OF LEARNING DISABILITIES

What Are Learning Disabilities?

A learning disability (LD) is a label that is given to identify that the student has a difficult time learning and using certain skills. LD varies from one student to the next, and no two children who are identified with a learning disability necessarily share the same characteristics or have the same problems. One student identified with LD might have difficulty with reading comprehension and another student identified with the exact same label might have difficulties with remembering and applying the basic multiplication facts. The skills most often affected are reading, writing, listening, speaking, reasoning, and completing math computations.

The Individuals with Disabilities Education Act (IDEA, 2004) offers a more formal description, which includes the following definition of a "specific learning disability":

> (10) *Specific learning disability*—(i) *General. Specific learning disability* means a disorder in one or more of the basic psychological processes involved in understanding or in using language, spoken or written, that may manifest itself in the imperfect ability to listen, think, speak, read, write, spell, or to do mathematical calculations, including conditions such as perceptual disabilities, brain injury, minimal brain dysfunction, dyslexia, and developmental aphasia.
>
> (ii) *Disorders not included.* Specific learning disability does not include learning problems that are primarily the result of visual, hearing, or motor disabilities, of intellectual disability, of emotional disturbance, or of environmental, cultural, or economic disadvantage. [34 CFR §300.8(c)(10)]

A learning disability is a neurological disorder in which the brain is wired a little differently than in other children. Children with learning disabilities can be as smart or smarter than their peers, but they may have difficulty with specific skills in areas such as reading, reasoning, spelling, writing, recalling, and/or organizing information. They most likely will not learn the same way other students learn, and conventional ways of instruction may not be effective.

A learning disability is a lifelong issue that doesn't have a cure or fix. Teachers and parents, however, can teach students with LD to be successful. The implementation of the right supports and interventions can help students with LD be very successful in school and as an adult.

What Teachers Need to Know About Learning Disabilities

Some facts about LD are very important to know and understand. First, according to the National Institutes of Health, about one in seven Americans have LD, which translates to about 15% of the population in the United States (LDOnline, 2010). Students with LD most commonly experience difficulties in reading and language skills. As many as 80% of students with LD have reading problems, and it is the number one area listed as a cause for referral. In addition, there is a hereditary link. It is often the case that more than one sibling has LD or a parent has LD. ADHD and LD often occur at the same time, but the two disorders are not the same.

There is no one characteristic that will enable a teacher to identify a student with LD. A child with a learning disability could have difficulties in any of the following areas:

- learning the alphabet, rhyming words, or connecting letters to their sounds;
- understanding what they read;
- spelling simple and complex words;
- the ability to write neatly or properly hold a pencil;
- following directions in and out of school;
- confusing math symbols, misreading numbers and letters of the alphabet;
- a limited vocabulary;
- managing social situations or expressing themselves; and
- performing multistep processes.

It is almost certain that a student will not have difficulties in all the areas or even most of them. However, if a student has a number of issues in and out of school, then parents and the teacher should consider the possibility that the student has a learning disability. Teachers and parents should be aware that the earlier an intervention is begun the more likely a student will reach academic success.

INCLUSIVE CLASSROOM STRATEGIES

Family Interventions

Students with LD are more successful when their parents and teachers work together. Cooperation and collaboration among parents and teachers depends on mutual respect (Mercer, Mercer, & Pullen, 2011). The following are recommendations that may nurture teacher-parent relationships:

◻ Provide parents with information about important activities and processes.

◻ Provide parents with training on how to tutor their child.

◻ Invite parents to volunteer in the classroom.

◻ Develop a communication system between the teacher and parents regarding homework.

◻ Communicate frequently with parents (i.e., notes home, phone calls, progress reports, etc.).

◻ Ask parents to help with academics by reading to the child nightly, reviewing math facts, signing homework, taking child to the library, etc.

◻ Invite parents to go on field trips or visit the classroom.

◻ Focus on listening to parents in an effort to understand their perspective and to show respect.

◻ Help parents become informed advocates for their child.

◻ Provide transportation and child-care services for parents to attend school meetings and events. (pp. 26–27)

Classroom Interventions

Planning activities for children with learning disabilities in an inclusive setting requires an action plan that enables the teacher to create a community of learners and provides a framework for making instructional decisions (Mercer & Pullen, 2009). Instructional decisions and activities often include reading. Thus, it is vital that teachers provide support for those students who are struggling to read.

Reading Interventions

Students with LD often struggle to read. In fact, it is one of the central difficulties of students with learning disabilities. Of those students with LD, more than 80% have reading problems (Lerner & Johns, 2009). According to the National Reading Panel (NRP, 2000), five essentials components of effective reading are:

1. phonological awareness training,
2. phonics instruction,
3. fluency instruction,
4. vocabulary instruction, and
5. comprehension instruction.

Discussed below are strategies that address each of these five areas. Figure 8 identifies the essential elements of reading.

Phonological awareness. Phonological awareness is a broad term that refers to a child's ability to recognize and manipulate the smallest units of sounds such as phonemes, syllables, and words. Phoneme awareness, a component of phono-

Essential Element of Reading	Definition
phonemic awareness	your ability to hear, identify, and put together phonemes, which are the smallest units of sound
phonics	the system of teaching the relationships between letters and sounds in language
reading fluency	the ability to read phrases and sentences smoothly and with a reasonable speed, and, at the same time, understand what it is that you are reading
vocabulary	the words you must know in order to communicate effectively
reading comprehension	the ability to understand what you are reading

Figure 8. Essential elements of reading. From *Take Control of Dyslexia and Other Reading Difficulties: The Ultimate Guide for Kids* (p. 14) by J. E. Fisher and J. Price, 2012, Waco, TX: Prufrock Press. Copyright 2012 Prufrock Press. Reprinted with permission.

logical awareness, is the ability to recognize and manipulate the smallest unit of sound, phonemes (Wendling & Mather, 2009). Phonemic awareness is demonstrated when a child exhibits the ability to hear, identify, and manipulate individual sounds.

The Say-It-and-Move-It Activity (Blachman, 1991) is a phonological segmentation task in which children are taught to represents sounds in words by using manipulatives (such as a disk, button, or tile). For each sound presented, the child represents (i.e., moves) the manipulative on a card. The card is divided in half. The top half is the storage area for the manipulative. The bottom half is an arrow pointing from left to right. If the teacher says "Show me the *a*," the child moves the manipulative from the top half of the card to the lefthand end of the arrow and says the sound. After demonstrating mastery of one phoneme, the teacher progresses to two phoneme words (*up, it, on*) and three-phoneme words (*sun, fat, zip*).

Phonics. Phonics instruction begins with printed letters and words and their corresponding sounds. Phonics instruction focuses on helping children learn the relationship between written letters and spoken sounds. It teaches students the alphabetic principal that, in turn, improves reading and spelling skills (Mercer et al., 2011). Phonics instruction can be integrated into a balanced reading program. Moreover, many basal reading programs are incorporating a phonics-based approach to teaching reading.

Fluency. Fluency is the ability to read quickly and accurately. Extensive research has been conducted in the area of fluency. Of the strategies that have been researched, repeated and monitored oral readings have been found to improve reading fluency and overall reading achievement (NRP, 2000). Reading fluency, however, does not indicate if comprehension is accurate or substantial for the student. Just because a student can read fast and accurately doesn't mean that she can comprehend the material. Teachers in inclusive classrooms should also address comprehension of reading material, as that should be the overall goal regarding reading understanding.

It is important for educators to use strategies that incorporate active student participation within their intervention. Repeated readings offer that participation. Repeated and monitored oral reading (i.e., repeated readings) require students to read aloud short, meaningful passages several times while being monitored by their teacher. Specifically, students read and reread a text a certain number of times or until a certain level of fluency is reached. Typically, a satisfactory level of fluency is 80 to 100 words correct per minute with greater than 95% accuracy (Mercer & Pullen, 2009). After obtaining these criteria, the procedure is repeated with a new passage. Four rereadings are sufficient for most students (Armbruster, Lehr, & Osborn, 2001).

By combining repeated readings and other effective practices, students can increase their reading abilities and therefore increase probable success in other academic areas. According to Armbruster et al. (2001), there are no easy answers or quick solutions for improving reading achievement: "As many teachers and parents will attest, reading failure has exacted a tremendous long-term consequence for children's developing self-confidence and motivation to learn, as well as their later school performance" (p. 1).

Vocabulary. Learning new vocabulary is a common demand in classrooms. For example, science teachers frequently expect students to remember the meanings of abstract words, such as *inertia* and *prototype*. Similar expectations are met in social studies, literature, and math. However, students who are struggling to read often have difficulty remembering vocabulary words and their meanings. Moreover, these students frequently use ineffective strategies that lead to frustration and failure. One example of an ineffective strategy is rote recitation to remember the meaning of the word. The University of Kansas Center for Research on Learning (KU-CRL) has developed the LINCS Strategy to enable students to learn new vocabulary words by using a memory-enhancement technique (i.e., mnemonic device; Ellis, 1992). The steps of LINCS are:

L = List the Parts
I = Identify a Reminding Word
N = Note a LINCing Story
C = Create a LINCing Picture
S = Self-Test

These steps cue the student to focus on the important elements of the vocabulary word; use keyword mnemonic devices, mnemonic stories, visual imagery, and associations paired with prior knowledge; and self-evaluation to enhance their memory of the meaning of the word (Ellis, 1992).

Comprehension. Comprehension is an active process that enables the child to gain meaning from the words being read. It is the reason for reading and requires thoughtful and purposeful interaction with the text (Mercer et al., 2011). The National Reading Panel (2000) noted two key findings from results of its research: Text comprehension can be improved by instruction that helps readers use specific comprehension strategies, and students can be taught comprehension strategies (Armbruster et al., 2001).

For more than 20 years, a major research area in reading has been comprehension strategy instruction. The principle behind comprehension strategy instruction is that reading comprehension can be improved by teaching students specific cognitive strategies to use when they encounter roadblocks in understanding text as they read. Original research in this area used a "direct instruction" model. In direct instruction models, educators teach specific strategies or a set of strategies with the expectation that students self-regulate their reading using the strategies. Because being a proficient reader involves constant adaptation of many cognitive processes, teachers must know a variety of strategies for reading instruction and be skilled in identifying the most effective strategies for students with LDs in reading. The NRP (2000) drew three conclusions from research on comprehension instruction. First, reading comprehension strategies involving children who are developing typically has been the most widely researched area within comprehension instruction. Second, for children who are not disabled, teaching reading comprehension strategies has led to an increased awareness and use of such strategies, improved performance on commonly used comprehension measures, and, sometimes, increased scores on standardized tests of reading. Finally, the third finding of the panel was that more research is needed that focuses on ways that reading comprehension strategies can be taught within the natural environments (versus laboratory-type settings) of classrooms for all students, not just for students who are achieving without difficulties.

Additionally, the NRP (2000) drew two conclusions from the review of research on teacher preparation and comprehension strategies. One of the conclusions from the review of research was that teachers can learn to teach comprehension strategies effectively. After such instruction, the teacher's proficiency is greater, which leads to improved student performance on the awareness and use of such strategies, improved performance on a commonly used comprehension measure, and, sometimes, higher scores on standardized tests of reading. Considering the first finding of teacher preparation and strategy instruction, Vaughn and Coleman (2004) conducted a study that involved 12 teachers from two schools. The purposes of the study were to determine the extent that teachers would learn and implement a specific strategy taught by a mentor, and teachers' perceptions of satisfaction after working collaboratively with a fellow teacher to enhance teaching a specific strategy. Based on the data collected, teachers in the study reported that they liked working with a colleague to learn or teach an instructional strategy. Further, mentor teachers liked working with other teachers. Finally, researchers' observations revealed that mentees used the strategy and mentors maintained use of the strategy.

In a related study, researchers examined five intervention and five control teachers and their classes, divided among five different schools. Intervention teachers attended a Collaborative Strategic Reading (CSR) professional development workshop and were provided continual support throughout the year-long study. Students in CSR classrooms improved in reading comprehension as compared to the control group. With the exception of one teacher, case studies reflect that students' comprehension gains were associated with the quality of CSR implementation (Klingner, Vaughn, Arguelles, Hughes & Leftwich, 2004).

Research indicates that good comprehension requires the use of a variety of strategies. Good readers use strategies automatically, but readers who are struggling require explicit strategy instruction that includes how, when, where, and why to use each strategy (Wendling & Mather, 2009). The TELLS procedure developed by Idol-Maestas (1985) is a prereading strategy to boost comprehension. Prior to reading, students are taught to look at the *Title* and form clues as to what the passage/material is covering. The second step, *Examine*, instructs students to skim pages for clues about the text. In the third step students *Look* for important words (i.e., words that are used often), and in the fourth step, they *Look* for hard words (i.e., unfamiliar words) and find their meanings. During the final step, *Setting*, readers skim the passage for clues about the setting.

Memory strategies. Learning and remembering information is a part of life. As such, memory plays a critical role in all academic learning (Dehn, 2006). Children with LD often experience weaknesses when required to learn and remember school-related information. This has led to an increased concern for how best to help these children. Methods for improving memory have existed for many years, but one strategy in particular, mnemonic strategy instruction, has been proven effective when learning and remembering information.

Mnemonic strategy instruction links new information with prior knowledge using visual and auditory cues. One example of mnemonic strategy instruction is the *Keyword Method.* The keyword method provides encoding and retrieval features and interactive elaborations. This strategy is effective when information is newly introduced, unfamiliar, and requires a link to familiar information (Mastropieri et al., 2005). Children might use this strategy when learning foreign words, scientific terms, or content-related vocabulary (Mather & Jaffe, 2002). To implement the keyword method, unfamiliar information is made concrete by changing the new unfamiliar word into a similar sounding but concrete word (Mastropieri et al., 2005). In addition, the keyword should be an easily pictured, tangible object. For example, a child who wants to remember the capital of Peru might think of a parrot as the keyword for Peru and lima beans for the capital of Lima. The child would then create a mental image in his or her head of a parrot eating lima beans. When taking a test that asks for the capital of Peru, the child would think of the parrot eating lima beans, thus remembering Lima as the capital of Peru (Mather & Jaffe, 2002).

Because mnemonic strategies are versatile, they can be used in many ways to help facilitate learning unfamiliar information. One technique is combining keywords with pegwords. Pegwords are used when children need to remember lists of information that are numbered or ordered. In the pegword method, the pegword must rhyme with the number and an associated picture. For example, one is bun, two is glue, three is tree, four is floor, five is dive, six is bricks, seven is heaven, eight is gate, nine is line, and 10 is tent (Mastropieri et al., 2005; Mather & Jaffe, 2002). Pegwords are generally easy for students with LD to learn. After learning the pegword method, students substitute a pegword for a number within interactive illustrations to learn new information. For example, to help remember that spiders have eight legs, a teacher might show a picture of a spider spinning a web on a gate, the pegword for eight (Mather & Jaffe, 2002).

First-letter mnemonic strategy is another technique that can help children remember and recall facts and information. For first-letter mnemonics to be effective, information must be familiar and meaningful to the child. An example of first letter mnemonic is FOIL for learning the order of operations when multiplying two binomials (First terms, Outer terms, Inner terms, Last terms). Another example of first-letter mnemonic strategy is the use of an acrostic. A child would take the first letters of the words to be remembered and make up an easy-to-remember sentence (Mather & Jaffe, 2002). For example, to learn the order of cardinal directions when studying map skills, a child takes the first letters of "Never Eat Sour Watermelons" and places them on a map moving from the top of the map clockwise to represent north, east, south, and west.

APPLYING THE STRATEGIES

Yojanna attends class in a general education classroom. Her teacher, Ms. Smyth, is also concerned about Yojanna's reading ability and has referred her to the student support team for a possible special education evaluation. Ms. Smyth conducts small-group instruction with Yojanna but has not seen measurable improvements in her reading ability. Yojanna has the reading ability of a second grader, with a reading fluency rate of 95 words correct per minute. Her reading skill is impacting her ability to be successful in other academic areas.

Working With the Whole Class

The following are specific strategies that Ms. Smyth implemented in her inclusive classroom to assist Yojanna and other students who were struggling to read:

◻ *Provide vocabulary instruction.* Ms. Smyth realized that her children who were struggling to read needed explicit vocabulary instruction. Prior to reading assignments, Ms. Smyth pretaught key vocabulary words that were unfamiliar. In the process, she related the vocabulary words to the children's background knowledge and experiences.

◻ *Use recorded stories.* Ms. Smyth encouraged all children, as well as Yojanna, to use the listening center to listen to stories and books. Listening to stories is an effective strategy for developing vocabulary. By listening to stories, children are exposed to words, language, and story structures that cannot be obtained through reading (Wendling & Mather, 2009).

◻ *Use graphic organizers.* Graphic organizers provide a visual tool to help children acquire new vocabulary and connect concepts. A specific type of graphic organizer that Ms. Smyth used in her classroom was word webs. Word webs expand word knowledge by asking the child to think of related words for target words. The target word is placed in the center of the web and related words are placed in bubbles connected by lines from the center (Wendling & Mather, 2009).

Working With Individual Children

The majority of children in special education are children who have learning disabilities. As there is a wide range of learning disabilities, it is important that teachers implement a variety of strategies that address different needs. The following are strategies that Ms. Smyth implemented for Yojanna:

◻ *Refer for evaluation.* Ms. Smyth referred Yojanna to the student support team (i.e., Response to Intervention team) in order to obtain more information about her reading abilities. Even though Ms. Smyth frequently conducted curriculum-based measures and implemented reading strategies in the classroom, Yojanna did not seem to be progressing.

◻ *Practice repeated readings.* During small-group instruction, Ms. Smyth would conduct repeated readings with Yojanna. Ms. Smyth also sent the passages home with Yojanna so that she could read them to her parents in the evenings, providing her with more practice opportunities.

◻ *Use LINCS strategy.* In addition to preteaching key vocabulary words, Ms. Smyth used the LINCS strategy to help Yojanna retain the meanings of vocabulary words that were presented in her reading assignments.

◻ *Use mnemonics devices.* Because Yojanna struggled with remembering information and being able to retrieve stored information, Ms. Smyth taught Yojanna mnemonic devices. For example, when studying the Great Lakes, Ms. Smyth taught Yojanna the acronym HOMES: Huron, Ontario, Michigan, Erie, and Superior.

¤ *Refer for counseling support.* Due to the ongoing custody battle, Ms. Smyth referred Yojanna to the school counselor where she could have a safe place to talk about her family and her feelings.

¤ *Teach comprehension strategies.* In conjunction with strategies to increase Yojanna's reading fluency, Ms. Smyth taught Yojanna the *TELLS* procedure to help her gain meaning from the reading assignments that she read or listened to in class.

Working With Families

The following are specific strategies that Ms. Smyth used to work with Yojanna and her family:

¤ *Use recorded texts.* Ms. Smyth knew that a slow reading rate had a profound negative effect on Yojanna's reading comprehension. Thus, she provided Yojanna with recorded texts of required readings so that she could listen to them at home, enabling her to participate in class discussions and activities the following day.

¤ *Communicate.* Ms. Smyth was aware of the joint educational rights of Yojanna's family and communicated frequently with both sets of Yojanna's parents regarding her educational progress.

¤ *Use repeated readings.* Ms. Smyth asked Yojanna's parents to listen to Yojanna read passages that were read during small-group instruction. This allowed Yojanna multiple practice opportunities of a single passage. Ms. Smyth also taught Yojanna's parents how to monitor and provide corrective feedback.

IF YOU WANT TO KNOW MORE

Council for Learning Disabilities—http://www.cldinternational.org
Learning Disabilities Association of America—http://www.ldanatl.org
LDOnline—http://www.ldonline.org
National Center for Learning Disabilities—http://www.ncld.org

6

Coleman

A STUDENT WITH AN EMOTIONAL OR BEHAVIORAL DISORDER

Coleman is a 7-year-old child who has been identified as a student with an emotional or behavioral disorder. Most of Coleman's school day is in the general education classroom. However, he attends a behavior intervention support class in a special education setting and is monitored by the behavior intervention special education teacher, Mr. Peck.

Coleman resides with his biological mother. His mother is involved in Coleman's education. She attends most of Coleman's IEP meetings and is concerned about his educational progress. His father is present for some of Coleman's life. Child protective services have been investigating the family regarding alleged child abuse against Coleman.

Coleman's relationship with his teacher, Ms. Rice, is mostly confrontational. However, Mr. Peck and Coleman have formed a positive student-teacher relationship. Mr. Peck makes it a point to assist Coleman as much as possible by providing a safe location when Coleman needs a trusted adult to talk to and being a sounding board for him when he needs someone to listen to him. In addition, Mr. Peck consults with Ms. Rice about Coleman's behavior and strategies that they might implement.

Recently, Coleman's inappropriate behaviors have increased to the point that Ms. Rice is concerned that his behaviors are interfering with his learning and with the other students' learning in the classroom. Coleman has repeatedly been sent to the assistant principal's office for such things as refusing to work in class, disruptive behavior during class (singing, shouting, and making rude noises), and use of foul language. An IEP meeting has been scheduled to discuss Ms. Rice's concerns.

OVERVIEW OF EMOTIONAL OR BEHAVIORAL DISORDERS

What are Emotional or Behavioral Disorders?

How many students have emotional or behavioral disorders (EBD)? Estimates indicate that from 6% to 10% of students have some form of EBD that may require special education and therapy. An emotional or behavioral disorder is characterized by a student exhibiting inappropriate or disruptive behavior on a consistent basis. This behavior then affects a child's performance in academic and social tasks, but there is not an intellectual basis or cause. Students with EBD typically exhibit average to above average intelligence and are perfectly capable of learning at their grade level, but their behavior often impedes learning.

In order for a student to be identified as EBD, there are four key concepts that must be considered. The first is that the student exhibits social, emotional, or behavioral functioning that is very different from that of their peer group. This behavior is generally different from those behaviors that are accepted and age appropriate, and it adversely affects a child's academic progress, classroom adjustment, social relationships, self-care, vocational skills, or personal adjustment. Second, the behaviors are severe, chronic, and frequent, and in addition to occurring at school, they also are exhibited in at least one other setting. Third, the IEP team uses a variety of sources of information, such as interviews, observations, and a records review of any past information, including any documented interventions that previous teachers have implemented. Finally, the IEP team does not identify or refuse to identify a student as EBD solely on some other situation (e.g., social maladjustment and cultural deprivation; Wisconsin Department of Public Instruction, n.d.). All of these aspects need to be taken into account when considering a student and identifying him or her with EBD.

What Teachers Need to Know About Emotional or Behavioral Disorders

The typical elementary teacher has probably not received much, if any, education on students with EBD. EBD can be broken into three different categories, each with different characteristics. The categories include internalizing behaviors (e.g., depression, anxiety, shyness, and self-criticism), externalizing behaviors (e.g., defiance, impatience, and agitation), and conduct disorders (e.g., defiance and aggressiveness). To properly serve students with EBD, a continuum of educational placements is necessary. General education classrooms where teachers implement supplementary aids and services are appropriate for some students. Other students with EBD may require self-contained (i.e., a separate class in the building with just students with EBD and a special education teacher) or pullout programming (i.e., students go to another classroom with support from a special educator) for all or part of their school day. Schools are also developing positive behavior intervention plans (BIPs) as part of the IEP when a student's behavior impacts his or her learning or that of others. This plan looks at current behavior and functioning and how a student can work on improving in school. The emphasis is on positive interventions and strategies to promote acceptable behaviors versus the behaviors the student is currently exhibiting.

INCLUSIVE CLASSROOM STRATEGIES

Family Interventions

It is important for educators to remember that families are families first and that their status of having a child with an emotional behavioral disorder is secondary. It is also important to recognize that educators benefit from developing and nurturing a relationship with the parents and families of the children in their classrooms (Wheeler & Richey, 2010). One way to facilitate a collaborative relationship is through family-centered approaches. Family-centered approaches are models in which professionals actively encourage families to be involved in developing programs for their children. Further, family-centered models reflect a change from viewing parents as passive recipients of professional advice to viewing them as equal partners in the educational process (Hallahan, Kauffman, & Pullen, 2012).

Lucyshym, Blumberg, and Kayser (2000) recommended three suggestions in supporting the role of families who have children with behavior problems:

- Provide family-centered, home-based positive behavior support services.
- Expand the unit of analysis and intervention to focus on family routines.
- Teach professionals to build collaborative partnerships.

Classroom Interventions

Teachers will likely encounter students with EBD in their classrooms. It is also likely that many teachers will observe behavior problems typically associated with EBD in a number of children with and without disabilities (Farley, Torres, Wailehua, & Cook, 2012). Thus, it is important that teachers implement evidence-based practices that have been proven to work when dealing with problematic behaviors.

Student-Teacher Relationship

A student's success depends on positive learning environments and multiple opportunities in class to experience academic and behavioral achievements. If a teacher has a good relationship with students, then they are more likely to follow the rules and procedures and accept consequences for behavior. Without a good relationship, students are more inclined to resist the rules and procedures of the classroom and more likely to oppose disciplinary actions (Marzano, Marzano, & Pickering, 2003).

One major obstacle in helping students experience academic and behavioral achievements is the relationship between teachers and their students with EBD (Doll, Spies, LeClair, Kurien, & Foley, 2010). Sutherland, Lewis-Palmer, Stichter, and Morgan (2008) cautioned that because students with EBD often display both learning and behavioral issues, providing effective instruction is often difficult for teachers to accomplish. In fact, a negative relationship between a teacher and student with behavioral problems greatly contributes to poor academics and behavioral outcomes altogether. Students who lack academic interactions with their teachers ultimately are exposed to a lesser degree of effective instruction when compared to their peers. Without effective instruction, teachers fail to provide access to praise to those students with behavioral difficulties. For students with behavioral difficulties to become adept in social-emotional learning, they must receive positive learning and social opportunities in school.

Further, it is important that case-management decisions (i.e., assigning students to special education teachers) be made from the perspective of the teacher-student relationship, especially in schools that have multiple special education teachers. Rueter and Trice (2011) noted that, "Best practice and common sense dictates that these case-management decisions are made individually from the perspective of the teacher and student relationship rather than the convenience of the school" (p. 38).

Positive Behavior Intervention Supports

Schools can promote student success by setting clear social expectations. To meet the needs of all students on the continuum, a system of behavioral expectations is outlined and includes levels of Positive Behavior Intervention Support (PBIS). These elements of PBIS are usually devised by creating support for the whole group while also allowing a range of increasing amounts of intervention to take place based on student need and response (Turnbull, Turnbull, Erwin, & Soodak, 2006).

By creating and providing multitiered levels of support, schools and teachers are more equipped to meet the needs of students with behavioral challenges. Students with EBD require the most intense support to address behavioral, social, and academic deficits. Assessing the function of their behaviors is a key factor to designing effective intervention strategies. One approach is to use a functional assessment-based intervention with its ability to individualize and tailor interventions for each student's needs (Lane et al., 2009). More precisely, the function of a student's behavior must first be ascertained by using a functional behavior assessment (FBA; Schoenfeld & Konopasek, 2007).

An FBA is the process of gathering and analyzing information about a student's behavior and accompanying circumstances in order to determine the purpose or intent of the actions. This investigation is designed to help educators: (a) determine the appropriateness of the student's present educational placement and services and whether changes would help the student to display more acceptable behavior, (b) identify positive interventions that would reduce the undesirable behavior, and (c) identify appropriate behaviors to be substituted in place of the inappropriate ones. An FBA is conducted to see why a student is exhibiting a specific behavior and what can be done to reduce the occurrence of the behavior. By implementing the FBA process, the teacher in the inclusive classroom will be better able to understand if there is something he or she is doing to promote the behavior and what can be done to reduce or replace the negative behavior. Figure 9 provides an excellent example of an FBA worksheet.

Behavior Intervention Plans

After the FBA has been conducted, the behavior intervention plan (BIP) may be developed to meet the social, emotional, academic, behavioral, and transition needs of the individual student with challenges. The BIP identifies which behaviors will be increased, decreased, and maintained. Specific intervention strategies, both proactive and reactive, should be explicitly stated. Interventions should focus on the direct needs of the student and identify the team members who will monitor and adjust behavioral goals as the student works toward mastery. Furthermore, rather than thinking of behavioral intervention as a punishment

Functional Behavior Assessment

Student:	Grade:	Date:

A. FBA TEAM MEMBERS

Please provide your name and title.

_____

_____

_____

_____

_____

_____

_____

B. SOURCES OF INFORMATION

Please select the sources used:
- ❏ Anecdotal information provided by parents
- ❏ Diagnostic evaluation(s) completed by:
  - ❏ School district
  - ❏ Outside agency
- ❏ Interviews completed by:
  - ❏ Parent
  - ❏ Student
  - ❏ Teacher
  - ❏ Other professional

- ❏ Classroom/school observation
- ❏ Attendance records
- ❏ Discipline records

- ❏ Behavior Rating Scales
- ❏ IEP(s)
- ❏ Other: _____
- ❏ Other: _____

C. STUDENT INFORMATION

1. Describe the student's behavioral strengths (i.e., positive interactions with staff and peers, accepts responsibility, ignores inappropriate behavior of peers, etc.).

2. Describe the things the student enjoys. For example, what makes him or her happy? What might someone do or provide that makes the child happy?

3. What has been tried in the past to change the problem behaviors?

D. DESCRIBE THE BEHAVIOR(S)

1. Describe the behaviors of concern. For each, define how it is performed; how often it occurs per day, week, or month; how long it lasts when it occurs; and the intensity at which it occurs (low, medium, high).

Figure 9. FBA worksheet. From "Behavioral Interventions for Children and Youth With Autism Spectrum Disorders" by S. J. Bock, J. P. Bakken, & N. Kempel-Michalak, In *Teaching Children With Autism in the General Classroom* (pp. 117–119) edited by V. G. Spencer and C. G. Simpson, 2009, Waco, TX: Prufrock Press. Copyright 2009 Prufrock Press. Reprinted with permission.

	Behavior	How is it performed?	How often?	How long?	Intensity?
1.					
2.					
3.					
4.					

2. Which of the behaviors described above occur together (i.e., occur at the same time, occur in a predictable chain, occur in response to the same situation)?

3. Prioritize the top two behavioral concerns listed above. These are the targeted behaviors you will refer to throughout this form.

Behavior	
1.	
2.	

E. EVENTS THAT MAY AFFECT THE BEHAVIOR

1. What medications does the child take and how do you believe these may affect his or her behavior?

2. List medical complications the child experiences that may affect his or her behavior (i.e., asthma, allergies, seizures).

3. Describe the sleep cycles of the child and the extent to which these may affect his or her behavior.

4. Describe the eating routines and diet of the child and the extent to which these routines may affect his or her behavior.

5. Briefly list the child's typical daily schedule of activities and how well he or she does within each activity.

Time	Activity	Child's Reaction

F. DEFINE EVENTS AND SITUATIONS THAT MAY TRIGGER THE BEHAVIOR(S)

6. **Time of Day:** *When* are the behaviors most and least likely to occur?
Most likely:

Least likely:

Figure 9. Continued.

7. **Settings:** *Where* are the behaviors most and least likely to occur?
Most likely:

Least likely:

8. **Social:** *With whom* are the behaviors most and least likely to occur?
Most likely:

Least likely:

9. **Activities:** *What* activities are most and least likely to produce the behaviors?
Most likely:

Least likely:

10.   **Antecedents:** Describe the relevant events that precede the target behavior.

11.   **Consequences:** Describe the result of the target behavior (i.e., what is the payoff for the student?).

12.   How much of a delay is there between the time the child engages in the behavior and when he or she gets the "payoff"? Is it immediate, a few seconds, or longer?

13.   What one thing could you do that would most likely make the problem behavior occur?

14.   What one thing could you do to make sure the problem behavior did not occur?

G. IDENTIFY THE FUNCTION OF THE TARGET BEHAVIOR

Using the prioritized behaviors from section D, define the function(s) you believe the behaviors serve for the child (i.e., what does he or she get and/or avoid by doing the behavior?). Think SEAT: sensory, escape, attention, tangible.

	Behavior	Function (What does he or she get? OR What exactly does he or she avoid?)
1.		
2.		
3.		

H. SUMMARY STATEMENTS

Setting Event	Antecedent	Behavior	Consequence	Function

Figure 9. Continued.

to the student, all stakeholders (i.e., student, parents, teachers) should regard the BIP as a positive way to help address specific areas in need of change and relate to short- and long-term goals that impact the student's future success. Clear and measurable steps should also be outlined with regard to how the BIP will be monitored, evaluated, and updated as the student masters his or her goals or as the plan needs to be adapted (Bauer, Keefe, & Shea, 2001; Overton, 2009).

Self-Management Interventions

Self-management interventions can help students with EBD practice appropriate academic behavior while learning self-management skills they do not currently possess (Mooney, Ryan, Uhing, Reid, & Epstein, 2005). Most of these interventions are created through collaborative efforts between teacher and student, where both parties contribute to the development and implementation of the strategy. Five types of self-management interventions that teachers might implement include: (a) self-monitoring, (b) self-evaluation, (c) self-instruction, (d) goal-setting, and (e) strategy instruction (Farley et al., 2012).

Students who use self-management techniques such as charting behaviors during a given period of time improve the likelihood of academic success. Further, educators who teach specific self-management strategies are more likely to have increased student outcomes and overall satisfaction with the learning process.

Figure 10 provides an overview of possible accommodations to use with children who may exhibit challenging behaviors.

APPLYING THE STRATEGIES

Coleman's relationship with his teacher, Ms. Rice, is mostly confrontational. However, Mr. Peck and Coleman have formed a positive student-teacher relationship. Mr. Peck makes it a point to assist Coleman as much as possible by providing a safe location when Coleman needs a trusted adult to talk to and being a sounding board for him when he needs someone to listen. In addition, Mr. Peck consults with Ms. Rice about Coleman's behavior and strategies that they might implement.

Recently, Coleman's behaviors have increased to the point that Ms. Rice is concerned that his behaviors are interfering with his learning and with the other students' learning in the classroom. Coleman has repeatedly been sent to the assistant principal's office for such things as refusing to work in class, disruptive behavior during class (singing, shouting, and making rude noises), and use of foul language. An IEP meeting has been scheduled to discuss Ms. Rice's concerns.

Tool 9.3: Possible Accommodations for Kids With Challenging Behavior

Timing

+ Extend time
+ Allow completion over several days
+ Adjust the order of tasks or tests

Presentation

+ Read aloud; indicate full text or partial text. Include use of technology that reads aloud
+ Enlarge print or clear print for reading material
+ Teach underlining and highlighting skills
+ Pair oral with visual cues
+ Give one direction at a time and check understanding
+ Simplify language used in directions
+ Shorten directions
+ Break down directions in bullet form
+ Repeat directions
+ Ask student to paraphrase or repeat direction

Environment

+ Limit or structure visuals posted on walls
+ Label materials clearly in organized fashion
+ Limit group noise
+ Be aware of lighting changes
+ Provide visually clear worksheets
+ Small-group testing
+ Test individually
+ Specify reduced ratio staff to student
+ Give preferential seating: front, near teacher, away from noisy machines, away from distracting peers, near study buddy
+ Increase distance between desks

Product

+ Shorten assignment expectation
+ Adjust workload: fewer problems, more practice problems, more enrichment, eliminate or reduce homework, specify time to work on homework
+ Break long-term or multistep tasks into component parts
+ Allow alternate product such as oral presentation of an essay, PowerPoint presentation, web-based product, illustrations
+ Adapt assignment to minimize writing (e.g., circle, cross out, write above line)
+ Allow student to orally dictate, with human scribe, recorder, or technology

Process

+ Establish routines and subroutines for structure and consistency
+ Provide visual schedule or written routines
+ Prepare child for changes in routine by practice, modeling, and discussion
+ Put student first in line
+ Give student a job between transitions
+ Provide closer supervision during transitions
+ Establish, teach, model, and post expectations
+ Provide movement breaks after or during seated work periods
+ Limit or remove distractions from tabletop and desktop
+ Shorten work periods

Figure 10. Possible accommodations for kids with challenging behaviors. From *School Success for Kids With Emotional and Behavioral Disorders* (pp. 204–206) by M. R. Davis, V. P. Culotta, E. A. Levine, and E. H. Rice, 2011, Waco, TX: Prufrock Press. Copyright 2011 Prufrock Press. Reprinted with permission.

Content and Study Skills
- Provide outline, syllabus, and study guides in advance of tests
- Allow open-notes or open-book tests
- Test one skill at a time
- Adjusted notetaking, use alternate forms for notes (e.g., fill in the blank, circle)
- Give student peer copy of notes
- Give student teacher copy of notes
- Limit copying from board or texts

Organization
- Spend time with student each period organizing materials
- Check homework and review mistakes individually
- Allow assignments to be e-mailed

Giftedness and Strengths
- Use adjusted questioning techniques
- Use areas of interest and strength to relate to task or curriculum
- Give child chances for leadership

Grading
- Do not downgrade for handwriting or spelling
- Permit extra credit assignments
- Permit re-revision after feedback
- Specify if effort is graded; whether student graded compared with himself, peers, or both; and how a parent should understand the grading

Figure 10. Continued.

Working With the Whole Class

Ms. Rice is concerned about the relationship that she has with Coleman. In an attempt to address this issue and the other behavioral concerns posed, she implemented the following strategies:

- *Seek out professional development.* Ms. Rice actively sought out professional development opportunities and trainings in working with children who had significant emotional or behavioral disorders. Through these trainings, she obtained knowledge and skills in fostering a supportive environment that addressed the needs of students in her classroom with EBD and problematic behaviors.

- *Implement positive behavior intervention supports in the classroom.* Ms. Rice implemented positive behavior intervention supports for all children in her classroom. Through this model, children know what is expected of them and are provided opportunities to learn these expectations. Moreover, behavior expectations are stated positively, and students are rewarded for following the expectations more than they are punished for not adhering to them (Wheeler & Richey, 2010).

- *Model self-management.* Because self-management of behaviors is important for all children to obtain, Ms. Rice modeled self-management techniques and strategies and worked with children who were struggling with behavior (not just Coleman) on individual self-management strategies.

Working With Individual Children

Ms. Rice used the following strategies when she was working with Coleman:

- *Collaborate.* Ms. Rice was aware that Mr. Peck and Coleman formed a positive teacher-student relationship. Accordingly, Ms. Rice consulted with Mr. Peck regularly to improve her relationship with Coleman. One strategy that Ms. Rice implemented was issuing "tickets" that Coleman could use to talk to her or to Mr. Peck about issues that he was experiencing.
- *Refer.* Due to the circumstances that Coleman was experiencing within his family, Ms. Rice referred Coleman to the school psychologist to help Coleman address issues that were occurring.
- *Maintain a behavior intervention plan.* At Coleman's IEP meeting, the team reviewed and updated Coleman's behavior intervention plan. Moreover, the team developed positive behavior intervention supports specifically for Coleman. For example, Coleman was allowed to use "tickets" that were issued by Ms. Rice to excuse himself from the classroom to talk to Mr. Peck when he was about to engage in problematic behaviors.
- *Implement a self-monitoring chart.* In conjunction with Mr. Peck, Ms. Rice worked with Coleman in implementing a self-monitoring chart so that Coleman could track his behaviors. The target behavior that Ms. Rice, Mr. Peck, and Coleman agreed to track was completion of assignments in class. At various intervals predetermined by Ms. Rice, Coleman charted his progress toward task completion.
- *Implement SLANT.* Ms. Rice taught Coleman the SLANT strategy to help increase his participation in class. SLANT is a Starter Strategy developed by The University of Kansas Center for Research on Learning. The SLANT strategy is designed to enable students to participate in class in appropriate and productive ways. The five steps of SLANT are:

S = Sit Up
L = Lean forward
A = Activate your thinking
N = Name the key information
T = Track the talker

The steps of SLANT cue the child to combine nonverbal, cognitive, and verbal behaviors to actively engage and participate in class discussions (Ellis, 1991).

Working With Families

Ms. Rice used several strategies to engage Coleman's family in his education and behavior at school:

- *Implement a family-centered approach.* Ms. Rice recognized the positive influence that Coleman's mother could have on Coleman's behavior in the classroom. Thus, Ms. Rice worked to implement a family-centered model that involved Coleman's mother in the educational process.

- *Communicate.* One of the keys to avoiding problems and misunderstandings is communication. It is vital that teachers receive information from parents and parents receive information from teachers. Parents know their child and have more invested in the child emotionally; they can be an invaluable source of information about the child's characteristics, interests, and preferred activities (Hallahan, Kauffman, & Pullen, 2012). By communicating with Coleman's mother, Ms. Rice fostered a relationship in which she could call his mother when particular concerns arose.

IF YOU WANT TO KNOW MORE

Emotional and Behavioral Disorders: The Special Ed Wiki—http://sped.wikidot.com/emotional-and-behavoioral-disorders

Teaching Students With Severe Emotional and Behavioral Disorders: Best Practices Guide to Intervention—http://www.k12.wa.us/SpecialEd/Families/pubdocs/bestpractices.pdf

Council for Children With Behavioral Disorders—http://www.ccbd.net/

7

Serena

A STUDENT WITH A SPEECH AND LANGUAGE IMPAIRMENT

Serena is a 5-year-old girl in kindergarten who has been diagnosed with a pervasive speech and language disorder. Prior to entering kindergarten, Serena received Early Childhood Intervention (ECI) for speech and language.

Serena's kindergarten teacher, Ms. Houston, is concerned that Serena is not making adequate progress in her language skills to prepare her for first grade. Serena entered kindergarten without the requisite readiness skills (able to recite the alphabet, count up to 10, and identify the letters in her name). Additionally, Serena has difficulty with naming common objects in her environment and is struggling to acquire language skills that are needed for academic success.

Serena lives in a single-parent household with her biological mother and 10-year-old brother. Serena's mom works at a local factory. Serena attends before- and after-school daycare due to her mother's work schedule. She is identified as economically disadvantaged. The family receives governmental food and housing assistance.

An IEP meeting is scheduled to discuss Serena's progress toward her speech goals and objectives.

OVERVIEW OF SPEECH AND LANGUAGE IMPAIRMENTS

What Are Speech and Language Impairments?

There are many kinds of speech and language disorders that can affect children. The Individuals with Disabilities Education Act (IDEA, 2004) defines the term "speech or language impairment" as "a communication disorder, such as stuttering, impaired articulation, a language impairment, or a voice impairment, that adversely affects a child's educational performance" [34 CFR §300.8(c)(11)]. There are four major areas that are affected: articulation, fluency, voice, and language. Articulation is a speech impairment in which the student produces sounds incorrectly (e.g., the student has difficulty articulating certain sounds of letters, such as "l" or "r," or the student has a lisp). For fluency disorders, the student's flow of speech is disrupted by sounds, syllables, and words that are repeated, prolonged, or avoided. The student may also experience blocks of silence or inappropriate inhalation, exhalation, or phonation patterns. Students with voice disorders can have problems with loudness, pitch, or resonance. Finally, students with language disorders have difficulty understanding what others say or problems expressing themselves to others.

What Teachers Need to Know About Speech and Language Impairments

Students with speech and language impairments will require services outside what is provided in the general curriculum. Through IDEA, special education and related services need to be made available free of charge to every eligible child with a disability, including preschoolers (ages 3–21). These services are specially designed to address the child's individual needs associated with the disability—in this case, speech or language impairments.

Many children are identified as having a speech or language impairment after they enter the public school system. A teacher may notice difficulties in a child's speech or communication skills and refer the child for evaluation. Parents may also ask to have their child evaluated. This evaluation is provided free by the public school system. If the child is found to have a disability under IDEA, such as a speech-language impairment, school staff will work with his or her parents to develop an IEP.

To become more knowledgeable, the teacher should learn as much as he or she can about the student's specific disability. Speech or language impairments differ considerably from one another, so it's important to know the specific impairment and how it affects the student's communication abilities. It is also important to make sure that needed accommodations are provided for classwork, homework, and testing. These specific aspects will help the student learn successfully. The teacher can also collaborate with other teachers (special education teacher and speech-language pathologist), who can help identify strategies for teaching and supporting the student, ways to adapt the curriculum, and how to address the student's IEP goals in the classroom. Lastly, the teacher must communicate with the student's parents to regularly share information about how the student is doing at school and at home.

INCLUSIVE CLASSROOM STRATEGIES

Family Interventions

Families of children with speech and language impairments can help increase typical language development in their young child by seeking out early intervention services. When determining whether a language difficulty is serious enough to require intervention, parents may want to consider the following three questions (Kuder, 1997):

◻ Is the language difficulty interfering with the child's ability to learn and/ or socialize?

◻ Do other children tease or reject the child because of his or her language difficulties?

◻ Does the child appear to be concerned about the problem?

Children with speech or language impairments are at an increased risk for developing reading disorders over typically developing students who have no history of speech or language impairments (Schuele, 2004). Thus, it is critical that children are identified early and are provided age-appropriate intervention services. Parents can facilitate this process by collaborating with teachers and speech language pathologists in mapping a course of action, which may include a speech and language assessment.

Speech and language assessments are important in identifying the underlying difficulties within the child's expressive language and/or receptive language. Assessments are designed to measure receptive language skills, expressive language skills, auditory skills, articulation and phonology, pragmatics, oral-motor functioning, voice quality, fluency, and general communication skills. The assessment process consists of informal measures (e.g., observations, interviews, work samples, etc.) and administration of norm-referenced standardized instruments. The results of the evaluation are used in developing the student's IEP (Simpson & Warner, 2010).

Classroom Interventions

Because classroom teachers are able to observe children for most of the school day, they are in the best position to identify children with possible speech and language difficulties. Children who have trouble answering questions, following directions or instructions, and using language to communicate with peers or teachers may be experiencing language problems (Kuder, 1997). Once the initial observations are conducted, teachers should seek the assistance of a speech-language pathologist. The recommendations that are provided are based on individually selected assessments targeting the specific nature of the speech or language impairment.

The following describe interventions for students who have been identified with speech or language impairments in an inclusive classroom setting.

Reading interventions. Reading proficiently requires students to draw upon basic language knowledge. Moreover, proficient reading requires that students integrate a variety of skills, such as word decoding and comprehension. Because students with speech or language impairments have problems in decoding and comprehension, they are at a greater risk for experiencing reading failure (Schuele, 2004). Interventions that may assist students with speech or language impairments to develop appropriate age-related reading skills include balanced reading interventions and explicit instruction in the alphabetic principle to develop phonemic awareness skills.

Balanced reading interventions provide students with an approach to reading that is balanced in three ways. First, it combines four distinct methodologies to reading instruction that emphasize instruction in phonics and sight words, reading comprehension, writing, and self-directed reading. Second, balanced reading interventions address silent reading and comprehension. Third, balanced approaches are teacher-centered and student-centered. That is, teachers control the selection of materials and support learning phonics, words, and reading with comprehension. Students control the selection of writing topics and content, as well as self-directed reading (Erickson, Koppenhaver, & Cunningham, 2006).

Instruction in the alphabetic principal is important for developing phonemic awareness skills. Moreover, instruction in letter-sound correspondence is strongly correlated to subsequent reading skills with correlation coefficients as high as .60. The most important phoneme-analysis skills are segmenting and blending (McGuinness, 2005). Blending (pushing the sounds together) is important for decoding or applying phonics skills to unknown or unfamiliar words. Segmentation (pulling the sounds apart) is important to encoding (spelling). These skills must be explicitly taught for children to acquire phonemic awareness skills (Wendling & Mather, 2009).

Augmentative and alternative communication. Augmentative and alternative communication (AAC) can be used as part of language interventions to help students develop their speech and language skills (Romski, Sevcik, Cheslock, & Barton, 2006). AAC includes all forms of communication that are used to express thoughts, needs, wants, and ideas, excluding the use of oral speech. People with severe speech or language problems rely on AAC to replace speech that is not functional or to supplement existing speech. Special augmentative aids or devices help individuals express themselves. These devices or aids can range from low-tech devices to high-tech computerized systems.

There are two options for students who have speech-language impairments: unaided communication and aided communication. Unaided communication relies on the body to convey messages. Examples include body language, gestures, and/or sign language. With aided communication, a student uses his or her body as well as tools or equipment. Aided communication devices can range from paper and pencil to picture exchange systems to devices that produce voice output systems (American Speech-Language-Hearing Association [ASHA], n.d.).

Graphic organizers. Graphic organizers help students create nonlinguistic representations (imagery) in organizing and producing written products. Graphic organizers combine the linguistic mode (words and phrases) and the nonlinguistic mode in that they use symbols and arrows to represent relationships among ideas. They can also be used as advanced organizers to assist students in using their background knowledge to learn new information (Marzano, Pickering, & Pollock, 2001).

Wait time. Wait time offers students with speech or language impairments additional time before responding in order to think about or formulate their response. Given its simplicity and ease of use in classrooms, wait time is a highly effective instructional strategy. Further, providing students with wait time has the potential of increasing the depth of responses given (Marzano et al., 2001).

APPLYING THE STRATEGIES

Serena's kindergarten teacher, Ms. Houston, is concerned that Serena is not making adequate progress in her language skills to prepare her for first grade. Serena entered kindergarten without the requisite readiness skills (able to recite the alphabet, count up to 10, and identify the letters in her name). Additionally, Serena has difficulty with naming common objects in her environment and is struggling to acquire language skills that are needed for academic success.

Working With the Whole Class

The following are specific strategies that Ms. Houston implemented in her inclusive classroom setting:

◻ *Increase opportunities for communication.* To help develop Serena's verbal communication skills, Ms. Houston provided Serena with interactive communication opportunities throughout the school day. For example, Ms. Houston organized cooperative group activities during which Serena could verbally communicate with peers she felt comfortable with.

◻ *Provide vocabulary instruction.* Ms. Houston followed the guidelines of the National Reading Panel findings related to vocabulary instruction: (a) vocabulary should be taught directly and indirectly, (b) words must be seen multiple times in multiple contexts, (c) language-rich environments foster incidental learning of vocabulary, (d) technology helps develop vocabulary, and (e) no one single method works best all of the time for teaching vocabulary (Wendling & Mather, 2009, p. 82).

◻ *Use recorded stories.* Ms. Houston encouraged all children, as well as Serena, to use the listening center to listen to stories and books. Listening to stories is an effective strategy for developing vocabulary. By listening to stories, children are exposed to words, language, and story structures that cannot be obtained through reading (Wendling & Mather, 2009).

◻ *Use a variety of communication strategies.* Ms. Houston used a variety of communication strategies when talking with the children in her class-room. Among the strategies Ms. Houston used were elaboration and open-ended questions. For example, instead of asking, "What is the title of this book?" Ms. Houston might say, "Tell me about this book."

Working With Individual Children

When working with children who have speech or language impairments, teachers should consult with the speech-language pathologist and the child's IEP. The following are strategies that Ms. Houston specifically implemented for Serena in the classroom:

◻ *Augmentative and alternative communication systems.* Because Serena's verbal communication skills were limited, Ms. Houston consulted the speech-language pathologist in implementing AAC systems and devices for Serena in the classroom. For example, the speech-language pathologist recommended the use of photo books to help increase Serena's language and vocabulary skills. In creating photo books for Serena, Ms. Houston took pictures of Serena involved in a field trip to the zoo. Once Ms. Houston printed out the pictures, she and Serena created the photo book. Because photo books are based on experiences that the child has had, the books are both meaningful and fun and provide a rich context for developing language and vocabulary skills.

☐ *Listen to Serena's responses.* Ms. Houston listened carefully to Serena. Even when she could not clearly understand what Serena was saying, Ms. Houston used nonverbal communication (body language and facial gestures) so that Serena was aware that what she was saying was important. Ms. Houston's efforts created a supportive environment in which Serena could use her verbal communication skills.

☐ *Provide instruction in alphabetic principle.* Ms. Houston provided explicit instruction in the alphabetic principle to help increase Serena's phonemic awareness skills. One strategy that Ms. Houston used was the Say-It-and-Move-It Activity. This phonological segmenting task teaches children to represent sounds with a manipulative such as a tile, disk, chip, or button. As the child hears each sound, they represent the sound with the manipulative (Kuder, 1997).

☐ *Consult with the speech-language pathologist.* Ms. Houston regularly met with the speech-language pathologist regarding Serena's progress toward her IEP goals and objectives. In addition, these meetings allowed Ms. Houston and the speech-language pathologist time to discuss interventions that had been tried in the classroom. By regularly meeting with the speech-language pathologist, Ms. Houston had a clearer understanding of what techniques and instructional strategies to use with Serena to help increase her speech-language skills.

Working With Families

Ms. Houston used the following strategies when working with Serena's family:

☐ *Develop a collaborative relationship.* Ms. Houston knew that in order for Serena to increase her language skills, she needed the support of Serena's mother. Ms. Houston called Serena's mother early in the school year to start developing a collaborative relationship. In addition, Ms. Houston frequently called Serena's mother about progress that Serena was making in the classroom.

☐ *Encourage families to work with children at home.* To help increase Serena's language skills, Ms. Houston encouraged Serena's mother to model appropriate language. One strategy that Ms. Houston specifically recommended was that Serena read classroom stories at home that she had read in class (repeated reading). Repeated readings of stories has been found to increase children's vocabulary, reading fluency, and comprehension skills.

IF YOU WANT TO KNOW MORE

American Speech-Language-Hearing Association: Speech and Language Disorders and Diseases—http://www.asha.org/public/speech/disorders

Delayed Speech or Language Development—http://kidshealth.org/parent/emotions/behavior/not_talk.html

Children's Speech Sound Disorders: Questions and Answers—http://speech-language-therapy.com/index.php?option=com_content&view=article&id=16:ssd&catid=11:admin&Itemid=120

Speech and Language Delay and Disorder: University of Michigan Health System—http://www.med.umich.edu/yourchild/topics/speech.htm

Speech and Language Impairments: National Dissemination Center for Children with Disabilities—http://nichcy.org/disability/specific/speechlanguage

Christy

A STUDENT WITH A HEARING IMPAIRMENT

As Christy and her mother enter the school building on the first day of school, a child approaches Christy and says, "Hello." However, Christy does not respond. Her mother says hello to the child and Christy smiles at her fellow schoolmate. When they find Christy's class, Christy takes her seat but does not interact with other classmates.

Mrs. Singleton, Christy's teacher, met with Christy's mother prior to the first day of school and is aware that Christy has a hearing impairment. She places Christy near the front of the room but notices that Christy is reluctant to join her peers during group activities. When one of her peers asks her to join the class on the carpet to listen to a story, Christy does not respond. Mrs. Singleton motions for Christy to join the rest of the class on the carpet.

OVERVIEW OF HEARING IMPAIRMENTS

What Are Hearing Impairments?

A hearing impairment is a permanent hearing loss or a decrease in hearing that is so significant it negatively affects a child's performance in school or her ability to learn new information. A hearing impairment signifies a full or partial loss of the ability to detect or discriminate sounds. The reason for this loss is the physiology, anatomy, or function of the ear. A hearing impairment can be described in terms of the degree of a hearing impairment, ranging from a mild hearing impairment to a profound hearing impairment, or type of hearing impairment (permanent [sensorineural], not permanent [conductive], or a combination of both [mixed loss]).

There are different degrees of hearing loss that children can experience, ranging from a slight hearing loss to a profound hearing loss. Loss of hearing is described in decibels (dB HL). See Clark (1981) and Figure 11 for more on the different degrees of hearing loss.

What Teachers Need to Know About Hearing Impairments

Because a student has a hearing impairment does not mean that she is deaf or cannot learn. See Figure 12 for how students may be impacted by their hearing loss in reference to individual sounds they may or may not hear. It is very important that the classroom teacher learns as much as he or she can about the student with a hearing impairment in order to fully meet her optimal instructional needs. Depending on the severity of the loss, the teacher may be impacted differently, and this knowledge may influence the way he or she plans, implements, and assesses instruction to the student. Likewise, it is also important to know if the student has a hearing aid or even a cochlear implant to aid her in hearing.

One student could have very limited hearing, making learning more difficult, and another student could be very high functioning such that the teacher might not even notice a discrepancy in learning. Depending on that information, the student may need to be seated in a particular place for her to hear best during instruction. Typically the front of the room is the best location, but each case is different. The student may also read speech and/or use sign language to communicate. If this is the case, the student may have an interpreter in the classroom with her to help her communicate and learn.

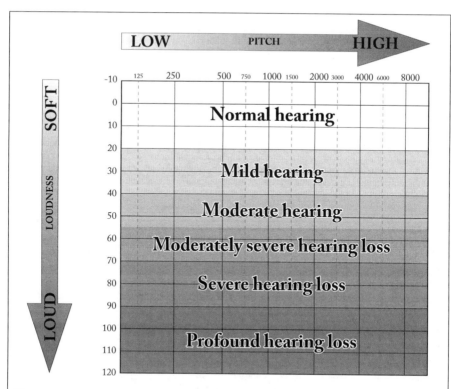

Figure 11. Degrees of hearing loss. From "Audiologist," by C. M. Schmidt, In *Collaboration: A Multidisciplinary Approach to Educating Students With Disabilities* (p. 214) edited by C. G. Simpson and J. P. Bakken, 2011, Waco, TX: Prufrock Press. Copyright 2011 Prufrock Press. Reprinted with permission.

Family Interventions

Families who have children with hearing impairments find many ways to communicate with their children, such as physical cues, gestures, assistive technology devices (e.g., hearing aid, cochlear implants, etc.), and American Sign Language. The preferred sign language system within the deaf community is the American Sign Language (National Association of the Deaf, n. d.). It is important for teachers, caregivers, and other people in the child's life to understand the communication system the family uses in order to ensure consistency across settings.

Classroom Interventions

Students with hearing impairments can benefit from instruction in the general education setting if specific accommodations are made. These accommodations will vary based on the severity of the hearing impairment and whether the child has interpreters who accompany him throughout the school day. Teachers who have a student with a hearing impairment in his or her class should pre-

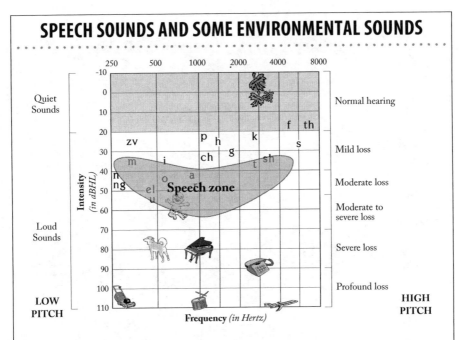

Figure 12. Speech and environmental sounds that can be heard with hearing impairments. From "Audiologist," by C. M. Schmidt, In *Collaboration: A Multidisclipinary Approach to Educating Students With Disabilities* (p. 216) edited by C. G. Simpson and J. P. Bakken, 2011, Waco, TX: Prufrock Press. Copyright 2011 Prufrock Press. Reprinted with permission.

pare in advance for emergency procedures. Many fire alarms are equipped with flashing lights that will alert children with hearing impairments. Also, a peer buddy can assist in emergency situations by passing along information from the announcement system (Mastropieri & Scruggs, 2010). In addition to these guidelines, teachers should consider the strategies in the following sections.

Physical Environment

Students with hearing impairments should be seated close to the teacher so that he or she can maximize their hearing and enable them to read speech. They should also be allowed to adjust their position in order to face other children who may be speaking (Mastropieri & Scruggs, 2010).

The environment should be adapted to reduce background noise. Suggestions include adding carpeting to the floor, covering the bottom of chair legs with rubber caps to reduce sound reverberation, installing small fiberglass panels at various wall locations to break up sound reflections (empty egg cartons can serve as a substitute), and adding (or closing) window shades or curtains to reduce reverberation, as windows are highly reflective of noise (Pakulski & Kaderavek, 2002).

Instruction

When providing instruction for a student who has a hearing impairment, technology—including hearing aids, closed captioning, computer-assisted instruction, and, when appropriate, FM systems—are very helpful. FM systems include a cordless microphone for teachers and receivers that attach to the child's hearing aids. When using FM systems, the teacher must pass the microphone to classmates who may be speaking so that they can also be heard (Mastropieri & Scruggs, 2010).

Before beginning instruction, teachers should gain the student's attention, provide outlines of the class lectures and discussion, and present materials in writing to the maximum extent possible. Hand signals or devices that signal transitions will help students with hearing impairments understand what comes next. Teachers should allow students with hearing impairments to repeat questions, answers, and concepts. When working with an interpreter, extra space for chairs or desks within close proximity of the student with a hearing impairment will need to be provided for the interpreter. Teachers will need to prepare the class for the interpreter and his or her role in the classroom. They should be sure to schedule time with the interpreter to review the classroom procedures, routines, and processes. Interpreters cannot proceed at the same rate as a verbal presentation, so teachers will need to slow the rate of presentation accordingly (Mastropieri & Scruggs, 2010).

Other suggestions for teachers include (Pakulski & Kaderavek, 2002):

- talking distinctly, not louder;
- using a slightly slower rate of speech and pausing between ideas;
- facing the students—teachers must be careful not to speak when facing the blackboard;
- being animate; using gestures and facial expressions;
- being lively; emphasizing important points and using inflections;
- keeping sentences short and relating back to the main idea;
- providing as many visual supports as possible (written outline, pictures, etc.); and
- rephrasing rather than repeating. (p. 101)

American Sign Language

Teachers can consider learning American Sign Language, or at least some of the most important signs that the child uses, and signs that are important in the classroom. Many universities and community colleges provide continuing education courses in American Sign Language. Also teachers can consider teaching the other children in the class the basic signs that the child with hearing impairment uses and signs that may be used in instruction. These signs can help facilitate communication, reducing the impact of a communication barrier between the teacher, the child with the hearing impairment, and her classmates (Simpson & Warner, 2010).

APPLYING THE STRATEGIES

> Mrs. Singleton, Christy's teacher, met with Christy's mother prior to the first day of school and is aware that Christy has a hearing impairment. She places Christy near the front of the room but notices that Christy is reluctant to join her peers during group activities. When one of her peers asks her to join the class on the carpet to listen to a story, Christy does not respond. Mrs. Singleton motions for Christy to join the rest of the class on the carpet.

Mrs. Singleton was aware that Christy would be placed in her classroom, so she was able to immediately prepare her room for Christy's arrival.

Working With the Whole Class

Mrs. Singleton used the following strategies to prepare her classroom:

- *Provide visual aids.* Mrs. Singleton used visual aids to demonstrate activities and routines in the class. She also created posters of key information and concepts with picture cues. During storytime, Mrs. Singleton seated Christy directly across from her so that Christy could see the illustrations in the story as Mrs. Singleton read the book to the class.
- *Use technology.* Because the school announcements were broadcast via the television set in the classroom, Mrs. Singleton worked with the technology department in securing closed captioning for her classroom. Mrs. Singleton also used computer-assisted instruction and an FM system for lessons and whole-group activities.
- *Use nonverbal communication.* Facial expressions and gestures can be paired with speech and are essential in communicating. Moreover, facial expressions and body language help to clarify the tone of the conversation (Simpson & Warner, 2010). Mrs. Singleton animated her speech and used body language when communicating with Christy.
- *Eliminate background noise.* Mrs. Singleton adapted her classroom so that it was friendly for Christy by eliminating as much of the background noise as possible. Mrs. Singleton used rugs and carpets on the floors and covered the windows with curtains to reduce reverberation.

Working With Individual Children

Mrs. Singleton provided the following accommodations and instructional strategies when working with Christy:

- *Provide optimal seating.* Mrs. Singleton positioned Christy's seat so that she could face Christy during lessons and activities. In addition, Mrs. Singleton kept her hands away from her face and used facial expressions and body language when speaking. Mrs. Singleton knew it was important for her to face Christy directly when giving directions or speaking to be sure that Christy was able to receive the message. She also allowed Christy, at her own discretion, to readjust her seat when other students were speaking.

- *Provide visual cues.* Mrs. Singleton paired her class lessons and discussions with visual cues, gestures, and concrete objects. She also prepared class posters of the routines and activities so that Christy could refer to them as often as she needed to.

- *Use sign language.* By working with Christy's family, Mrs. Singleton learned signs that Christy used to express her basic wants and needs. In addition to the personal signs that Mrs. Singleton learned from Christy and her family, Mrs. Singleton also learned signs that were used to indicate transitions, speaking quietly or louder, and frequently occurring words. In an attempt to facilitate communication with classmates, Mrs. Singleton encouraged Christy to teach her classmates to sign.

- *Provide lesson notes.* Prior to giving a lesson and/or class discussion, Mrs. Singleton provided Christy with an outline of the lesson. Christy was then able to follow along with the lesson and participate as an active learner.

- *Use assistive technology.* Mrs. Singleton used a variety of assistive technology devices in her classroom. Specifically, she worked with the technology department to provide closed captioning for announcements. Mrs. Singleton also supplemented class lectures and lessons with computer-assisted instruction and used an FM system that attached to Christy's hearing aids.

Working With Families

Mrs. Singleton used the following strategies when working with Christy's family:

- *Communicate with the family.* Mrs. Singleton talked to Christy's family about the communication system (i.e., American Sign Language and physical cues) that they used in the home. She also took the opportunity to learn basic signs that Christy and her family routinely used so that she could incorporate them into her classroom.

◻ *Build friendships.* Provide opportunities for families to meet other families in the school who have children with hearing impairments. These opportunities allow families to be active participants in the school environment and help facilitate reciprocal relationships across family units.

◻ *Encourage parents to be active participants in the school environment.* Parents of children with hearing impairments should be active participants in their child's school. Teachers should provide opportunities that allow parents to participate. For example, opportunities to be room mothers/fathers, volunteers for field trips, and have lunch at school with their child can help to open the doors for parents of a child with a hearing impairment to be an active participant in the child's school life.

IF YOU WANT TO KNOW MORE

Hearing Loss in Children: Centers for Disease Control and Prevention—http://www.cdc.gov/ncbddd/hearingloss/index.html

Causes of Hearing Loss in Children: American Speech-Language-Hearing Association—http://www.asha.org/public/hearing/disorders/causes.htm

Deafness and Hearing Loss: National Dissemination Center for Children with Disabilities—http://nichcy.org/disability/specific/hearingloss

Division for Communicative Disabilities and Deafness—http://www.dcdd.us

National Association of the Deaf—http://nad.org

LeBron

A STUDENT WITH A VISUAL IMPAIRMENT

Although LeBron, a fifth-grade student who has visual impairments, successfully navigates the school building, he still has difficulty getting where he needs to be on time. Mrs. Scott, LeBron's orientation and mobility specialist, works with LeBron weekly on strategies that he can use in navigating his environment, but it seems the school environment, children, and other factors interfere with LeBron's goal of on-time arrival to his classes. LeBron's teachers understand his late arrival, but they also realize that he is missing out on key instruction that is affecting his grades. In addition, LeBron must leave his regular classroom settings to go to the special education room in order to access print-to-speech software (i.e., Kurzweil 3000) for any reading he must do.

OVERVIEW OF VISUAL IMPAIRMENTS

What Are Visual Impairments?

At some point in their lives, many people have some type of vision problem. Some can no longer see objects far away, while others have problems reading what's close. For both of these conditions, people can use eyeglasses or contact lenses to help them see better. With severe or total loss of vision, vision can't be restored with eyeglasses or contact lenses.

Typically, vision is measured using a Snellen chart. A Snellen chart has letters of different sizes that are read, one eye at a time, from a distance of 20 feet. People with normal vision are able to read the 20-foot line at 20 feet (which is referred to as 20/20 vision). If at 20 feet the smallest readable letter is larger, vision is designated as the distance from the chart over the size of the smallest letter that can be read. Eye care professionals measure vision in many ways. One aspect is clarity or sharpness of vision. This indicates how well a person's central visual status is. Other terms that are used to reflect refractive errors individuals experience include nearsightedness, farsightedness, and astigmatism. Also, individuals do not just see straight ahead but around them, and this entire area of vision is called the visual field. Some people have good vision (i.e., see clearly) but have areas of reduced or no vision (blind spots) in parts of their visual field. Others have good vision in the center but poor vision around the edges (peripheral visual field). People with very poor vision may be able to count fingers only at a given distance from their eyes. There are five categories of vision as identified by the World Health Organization (WHO). See Table 6 for a description of the five categories.

The term visually impaired is used to describe any kind of vision loss, from a partial loss of vision where some things are seen to a total loss of vision (National Dissemination Center for Children with Disabilities, 2012). IDEA (2004) defined visual impairment as "an impairment in vision that, even with correction, adversely affects a child's educational performance. The term includes both partial sight and blindness" (34 CFR 300.7 (c)(13)). If a student is found to have a visual impairment, the IEP team must also determine whether the student has a need for special education.

Visual impairments include students who are: (a) totally blind—where the student cannot see anything and needs to learn through braille or other media; (b) legally blind—the student has less than 20/200 vision in the better eye or a very limited field of vision (20 degrees at its widest point); (c) low vision—student has a severe impairment and is unable to read the newspaper at a normal viewing distance, even with the aid of eyeglasses or contact lenses; and (d) partially sighted (student has some type of visual problem and needs special education services).

Table 6
CATEGORIES OF VISION LOSS

Level of Vision Loss	Visual Acuity
Low vision 1	20/70
Low vision 2	20/200
Blindness 3	20/400
Blindness 4	5/300
Blindness 5	No light perception at all

Teachers could have any of these students in the regular classroom, so they need to thoroughly educate themselves on visual impairments and how they can make the educational experience a successful one for students.

What Teachers Need to Know About Visual Impairments

Students who have a visual impairment should be assessed early, when applicable, to benefit from early intervention programs. Teachers need to be aware if a student is having difficulty seeing the board, reading, or working on the computer. Any sign that the student might be having difficulty seeing should be reported to his parents, who can then take the student for an eye exam.

For students with a documented visual impairment, technology can be very helpful. Computers and low-vision optical and video aids can enable many students with partial sight, low-vision, and blindness to participate in regular class activities. There are many computer programs to create braille from text as well as enlarge text, create different colors of text, and create outlines for academic use. The law also requires that schools provide accessible instructional materials to all students who need them. These materials can include books on tape/CD, braille books, and large print materials.

Students with visual impairments may also need help with special equipment and modifications in the regular curriculum. This equipment may emphasize vocation/career options, listening skills, orientation and mobility, daily living skills, and communication. These students may need help using their residual vision more efficiently and with special aids and materials so that they do not rely on others or technology for everything. Often students with other disabilities may also have a visual impairment. In these cases, there is a greater need for interdisciplinary approaches, and they may require greater emphasis on self-care and daily living skills to be more functional.

INCLUSIVE CLASSROOM STRATEGIES

Family Interventions

Professionals can support families with children with visual impairments by providing adequate instructional and related services such as orientation and mobility (O&M) training and assistive technology. Accordingly, professionals who are highly trained in the area of visual impairments will need to work very closely with families to provide services. The frequency, duration, and intensity of these services are likely to change as the child develops his or her independence and cognitive skills.

Classroom Interventions

A consistent and organized environment is critical for students who have visual impairments. Classroom teachers should ensure that all classrooms are organized and orderly and have clear and open walkways. In science classrooms that involve experiments, teachers should develop specific safety guidelines and assign sighted peer buddies to assist the student with visual impairments. Teachers should prepare in advance for emergency situations such as fire and tornado drills (Mastropieri & Scruggs, 2010). In addition to these guidelines, other strategies are included in the sections that follow.

Physical environment. Aisles and walkways must be clear and free of clutter. In addition, teachers can prepare the student in advance by familiarizing her with the physical arrangements of the classrooms that she will be attending and notifying the student in advance if there are any changes. Classroom teachers should consult with the visual impairments teacher and the orientation and mobility specialist regularly for their recommendations and suggestions about access to the environment. What may seem easily accessible to a sighted person may not be navigable for a student with visual impairments.

Assistive technology. Assistive technology is very useful when providing instruction for a student with visual impairments. Text-to-speech software and oral output devices enable students with visual impairments to access printed material. Software such as Kurzweil 3000 can access any type of information including printed or electronic material (even the Internet). Because it is highly flexible, Kurzweil 3000 can be used with any curriculum. After the material has been scanned, the program highlights and reads aloud each word to the student. This enables the student to engage with the text and allows access to the general education curriculum (Wendling & Mather, 2009).

Using braille. Students with visual impairments generally begin receiving braille instruction in conjunction with reading instruction when they start kindergarten. Braille resources are available through the American Printing House for the Blind (http://www.aph.org) and National Library Service for the Blind and Physically Handicapped (http://www.loc.gov/nls; Simpson & Warner, 2010).

Recorded texts and books. Audio copies of classroom texts and required readings are excellent resources. Students with visual impairments (and students with reading disabilities) can be issued a set of audio textbooks and can access the material independently by listening to the readings with a set of headphones in a listening center in the classroom. Learning Ally is a national nonprofit organization that provides textbooks for individuals who are unable to read standard print. Its extensive library has education books from upper elementary to postgraduate level (Wendling & Mather, 2009).

Instruction

When considering the way in which instruction is delivered, the following strategies can be employed: use of physical prompts, cueing, response time, and/ or a peer buddy system. Each individual student will have his own unique needs and must be assessed accordingly.

Physical prompts. Physical prompts, such as touching the student's elbow to cue her or using hand-over-hand formats, gain a student's attention. In addition, when teaching lessons, educators can use simultaneous touch and vision if the student has partial vision. If the student is currently using touch cues to identify objects in her environment, combining these cues with visual training to connect the visual images to already established tactile perceptions is good practice (Swift, Davidson, & Weems, 2008).

Cueing. Teachers should use explicit language when describing concepts, avoiding phrases that are vague, such as "over there," "almost," etc. Instead, use specific phrases such as "above your head" or the "folder that is on your desk"; in other words, identify exactly where something is (Mastropieri & Scruggs, 2010). In addition, verbal information describes what the student is seeing and feeling, and when walking with students who have visual impairments, it important to warn them of upcoming barriers in their environment, such as "two steps going down to the cafeteria" (Mastropieri & Scruggs, 2010).

Response time. Classroom teachers should allow adequate time for the student with visual impairments to respond and complete class activities. They may need to use speech-to-text software, braille, or enlarged print technology to access materials. Teachers need to remember that speech-to-text software, reading braille, and enlarged print take longer than reading regular print (Mastropieri & Scruggs,

2010; Swift et al., 2008). Moreover, students with visual impairments will also need extra time to complete exams and standardized tests.

Peer buddies. A sighted peer buddy can help the student who has visual impairments. The peer buddy can help with activities such as transitioning from one activity to another and navigating to and from places within the school building. Further, these activities may facilitate and open friendships among a larger group of peers.

Working With an Orientation and Mobility Specialist

Orientation and mobility (O&M) specialists are essential components of an IEP for students with visual impairments. From the moment students wake up in the morning to the time they go to bed, orientation and mobility is part of every activity and every environment. The amount of service provided to a student and the location of the services may impact the skills that are taught during the instructional sessions. For example, some O&M specialists are able to serve students both in the home and school environments, but this is not always the case. In many instances, students are provided this service only during the school day—and in increments as minimal as 45 minutes in length. This arrangement may be overwhelming for an O&M specialist.

In order to accomplish the student's goals in such little time, a team approach is necessary. Working as a member of a team—specifically, with the general and special education teachers in an inclusionary environment—allows a more holistic approach to meeting the student's needs. This approach requires sharing knowledge, experience, and expertise and acknowledging one's limitations and other people's contributions (Perla & Ducret, 1999). Thus, O&M specialists must work collaboratively with other service professionals to provide support in the home and school environment in order that the student can maneuver safely and efficiently throughout his environment (Horn, Chambers, & Salito, as cited in Raver, 2009).

APPLYING THE STRATEGIES

Mrs. Scott, LeBron's orientation and mobility specialist, works with LeBron weekly on strategies that he can use in navigating his environment, but it seems the school environment, children, and other factors interfere with LeBron's goal of on-time arrival to his classes. LeBron's teachers understand his late arrival, but they also realize that he is missing out on key instruction that is affecting his grades. In addition, LeBron must leave his regular classroom settings to go to the special education room in order to access print-to-speech software (i.e., Kurzweil 3000) for any reading he must do.

Mrs. Scott has been working with LeBron on orientation and mobility training throughout the school year. It has been a steady, but slow, process due to the congestion in the halls during passing periods. Mrs. Scott realizes that it is important for LeBron to participate in his classes from start to finish but also understands the logistics of navigating a busy school campus. Moreover, it appears that the school obtained only one site license for the Kurzweil 3000 software, and consequently LeBron misses additional instruction time so that he can access required readings. In an attempt to address these issues, the following accommodations and strategies were considered by Mrs. Scott and the IEP team.

Working With the Whole Class

LeBron's teachers used the following strategies within their classrooms:

◻ *Make accommodations for time.* Mrs. Scott met with each of LeBron's teachers to listen to their concerns about LeBron's arrival and early leaves from each of their respective classes. In hearing their perspectives, Mrs. Scott was better able to understand the importance of on-time arrival and departure. In response, Mrs. Scott and the IEP team built extra time into LeBron's schedule in the form of an "enrichment period" where LeBron could receive instruction that he may have missed while navigating the school building.

◻ *Make arrangements for physical needs.* LeBron's teachers consulted LeBron's visual instruction teacher and Mrs. Scott regarding the arrangement of their classrooms. Each teacher rearranged furniture so that there were open, accessible, and uncluttered walkways and aisles. In addition, when they rearranged the furniture in the classroom, they forewarned LeBron of the changes.

◻ *Provide a peer buddy.* LeBron's homeroom teacher assigned LeBron a peer buddy who had a similar schedule. LeBron's peer buddy assisted LeBron with transitions in the classroom, emergency situations, and during instructional activities. For example, LeBron's peer buddy read in-class assignments to LeBron so that he would not miss instructional time by leaving the classroom to access the Kurzweil 3000 software. Further, LeBron and his peer buddy became close friends, and, as a result, both children developed a wider social group both in and out of school.

□ *Provide audiotexts.* Upon learning that there were many organizations that provided audio textbooks for students who are visually impaired, LeBron's teachers were able to provide LeBron with a class set of audio textbooks, and they also provided LeBron with a set to take home. In addition, each of his teachers set up listening centers in their respective classrooms so that LeBron could listen to required readings.

Working With the Individual Child

LeBron's teachers used the following strategies with LeBron:

□ *Call the child by name.* This practice is essential to gain the attention of a student who has visual impairments. LeBron's teachers and classmates used this simple strategy when speaking to him.

□ *Allow for response time.* LeBron's teachers provided LeBron with additional time to respond and to complete class assignments.

□ *Provide physical prompts.* LeBron's teachers were trained to physically prompt (e.g., hand-over-hand assistance) LeBron when doing hands-on activities. This was especially important during science experiments and learning centers.

□ *Use assistive technology.* LeBron's teachers created listening centers in their classrooms so that LeBron could access audiotexts. They also worked with the special education administrative office in obtaining additional site licenses for speech-to-text software that LeBron used so that he could remain in class to complete reading assignments, rather than going to the special education classroom.

□ *Encourage use of vision.* LeBron's teachers encouraged LeBron to use what vision remained. Most children, even if diagnosed as legally blind, have some residual vision.

Working With Families

When working with families of children who have visual impairments, educators should consider the following recommendations:

□ *Make arrangements for physical needs.* Just like in the school environment, homes need to be organized, clear of clutter, and accessible for the child with visual impairments.

◻ *Encourage independence.* All children need to gain independence and participate in activities appropriate for their age. LeBron's parents were active in their local Special Olympics chapter, allowing LeBron to participate in a wide variety of sporting events.

◻ *Refer to an Orientation and Mobility specialist.* The O&M specialist worked with LeBron's family so that he could independently navigate his community (e.g., park, sidewalks, etc.). As a result, LeBron and his family participated in community-wide events and activities.

IF YOU WANT TO KNOW MORE

Foundation Fighting Blindness—http://www.blindness.org

National Association for Parents of Children with Visual Impairments—http://www.spedex.com/napvi

Blindness/Visual Impairment, National Dissemination Center for Children with Disabilities—http://nichcy.org/disability/specific/visualimpairment

Division on Visual Impairments—http://www.cecdvi.org

Learning Ally—https://www.learningally.org

10

Deserre

A STUDENT WITH AN
ORTHOPEDIC IMPAIRMENT

Deserre is a 9-year-old elementary school student who has cerebral palsy and who is wheelchair bound. Deserre began receiving services as an infant and toddler under Early Childhood Intervention and as a child with orthopedic impairment (i.e., cerebral palsy) under the Individuals With Disabilities Education Act when she was 3 years old. Deserre is included in the regular classroom for most of the school day. Ms. Bowden, her special education teacher, provides coteaching services in Deserre's general education math, social studies, science, and English language arts classes.

Various related service personnel routinely work with Deserre. She receives occupational therapy, physical therapy, speech and language services, and adaptive physical education in addition to the regular academic program. Deserre has enough functioning in her right hand so that she can operate the joystick to move her motorized wheelchair. Deserre requires head restraints in her wheelchair as she lacks the ability to hold her head in an upright position. She requires assistance with eating and uses adaptive eating utensils to feed herself. A female paraprofessional assists Deserre with her personal hygiene needs.

Deserre is functioning on grade level in reading and math and is thought to be of average intelligence, although this has not been substantiated with standardized intellectual measures. An IEP meeting is scheduled regarding Deserre's program and placement for next school year.

OVERVIEW OF ORTHOPEDIC IMPAIRMENTS

What Are Orthopedic Impairments?

An orthopedic impairment is defined as a severe impairment that adversely affects a child's educational performance. The term includes impairments caused by congenital anomaly (e.g., absence of some member or clubfoot), impairments caused by disease (e.g., bone tuberculosis or poliomyelitis), and impairments from other causes (e.g., fractures or burns that cause contractures, amputations, or cerebral palsy). Under IDEA (2004), an orthopedic impairment means a severe orthopedic impairment that adversely affects a child's educational performance.

Students may be born with or acquire problems with their bones, their joints, and/or their muscles. Orthopedic problems may result from surgeries, diseases, deformities, or injuries. Problems a child might be born with include osteogenesis imperfecta, joint deformities, muscular dystrophy, and cerebral palsy. Also included are injuries or surgeries that may result in the loss of a bone and/or muscle tissue and may include the amputation of a limb. Burns and broken bones can also result in damage to both bones and muscles and are included in this category.

What Teachers Need to Know About Orthopedic Impairments

Regarding a student with an orthopedic impairment, the specific impact on learning is contingent upon the disease, its severity, and individual factors. Two individuals with identical types of impairments may be quite different in terms of their abilities. In fact, many students with orthopedic impairments have no cognitive, learning, perceptual, language, or sensory issues. Sometimes teachers automatically associate having an orthopedic impairment with a cognitive disorder when, in fact, many students with orthopedic impairments have no cognitive impairment at all. (However, individuals with more severe neurological impairments will have a greater likelihood of additional impairments.) For most students with orthopedic impairments, the impact on learning is typically focused on accommodations necessary for students to have access to academic instruction.

Because each student is different, what the teacher does for each student will be different. Things that teacher can do to help the student include using visual aids; allowing for hands-on learning; building on the child's strengths; providing summaries, notes, and study guides; teaching classmates to help only when asked by the student with orthopedic impairments; making every activity accessible to the student; building an accepting environment in the classroom; and ensuring accessibility in and out of classroom. The classroom teacher may also want to speak with the student's parents for any additional insight into how the child learns or how he or she can best be accommodated in the classroom.

INCLUSIVE CLASSROOM STRATEGIES

Family Interventions

Families of children with orthopedic impairments often require related services for their children. Such services may include occupational therapy, physical therapy, speech and language therapy, and individual and family counseling. It is critical that the family and the many service providers communicate frequently with one another and work toward common goals that are established in the child's IEP.

Classroom Interventions

Teachers have an important role in developing and implementing strategies and interventions for children with orthopedic impairments. Many students who have orthopedic impairments use wheelchairs. With respect to students who have orthopedic impairments and are in wheelchairs, accessibility is paramount in establishing independence and facilitating full participation in the school environment. Accessibility is much more than being able to get through the door of a school building. It means being actively and meaningfully included in all facilities, services, and programs. It means being able to use materials and technology that are available to other students (Cox & Lynch, 2006).

In addition to the above guidelines, educators should consider the following interventions.

Physical environment. For students who are in wheelchairs, aisles and walkways should be free of clutter and wide enough for the student to maneuver his wheelchair. In addition, the student needs adequate space to complete assignments and participate in class activities. Teachers should frequently monitor the classroom to ensure that there are no books, backpacks, or other objects that may impede mobility (Mastropieri & Scruggs, 2010).

The occupational therapist, physical therapist, and student should be consulted regarding access issues in the common areas of the school. What may seem easily navigable for an able-bodied child may not be accessible for a student who is in a wheelchair. Student bathrooms must be equipped for wheelchairs, including sinks that the student can reach. Water fountains, cabinets, and doorknobs need to be accessible from the perspective of the student. If there are access issues, notify the principal of the school to investigate available solutions.

Emergency procedures. Plan for emergency procedures. Students who have orthopedic impairments, even those who are in wheelchairs, will need more time to get to safe locations. In addition, they may need specialized procedures for emergencies, such as fires or tornadoes. During drills in which students are required to exit the building, there may be mobility issues, especially if they are maneuvering through grassy areas. Pair an able-bodied peer or a staff member with the student who has orthopedic impairments during emergency situations to assist if needed. Teachers should outline emergency procedures in advance and practice them so that all students are well prepared (Mastropieri & Scruggs, 2010).

Assistive technology. Assistive technology (AT) devices can range from pencil grips to adaptive switches and complex computer software and hardware (Dove, 2012). Students with orthopedic impairments will use a variety of AT devices in order to access the curriculum and their environment. Common types of AT devices for children with orthopedic impairments are described below:

- *Maxi keyboard.* An oversized keyboard that allows students who cannot use a standard keyboard access to keyboarding capabilities. The keys are four times larger than that of a standard keyboard.
- *Touchpads.* Students who have some hand strength and finger dexterity touch the hardware device to enter information.
- *Trackballs.* A trackball allows children who have poor dexterity to control the cursor using the finger, thumb, or palm of their hands.
- *Joysticks.* Students with limited strength/mobility in their hands may use a joystick to control their wheelchair.
- *On screen keyboards, pointing devices, and switches.* A wide variety of adaptive equipment allows students with severe impairments to be able to access technology by moving their head or with light touch (Mates, 2004).
- *Adaptive switches.* Adaptive switches are oversized switches (about the size of the palm of an adult hand or larger) that allow students to operate objects and to turn items on and off.

Additional study time. Schools should schedule extra reading and instructional support time. In addition, students who have difficulty speaking will need additional time to respond. Be sure to provide sufficient wait time for the student to respond so that she is comfortable and does not feel rushed while responding (Mastropieri & Scruggs, 2010). Moreover, alternative response modes may be necessary for students with orthopedic impairments. That is, limit oral responses for students who have difficulty speaking by providing augmentative communication devices or by allowing students to respond with gestures or eye gazes.

Software support. Speech-to-text software and word prediction software may be needed for students who have orthopedic impairments to minimize the difficulty of producing assignments. In addition, consider assigning a peer buddy who can assist in the classroom, thereby enabling the student with an orthopedic impairment to take a more active role in the classroom. If a paraprofessional accompanies the student to the inclusive classroom, work closely with the paraprofessional to design effective modifications (Mastropieri & Scruggs, 2010).

Related services and adaptive physical education. Students with orthopedic impairments have unique physical needs. Related service professionals such as occupational therapists and physical therapists can help address the types of stretching and movement students may need during the school day and in their adaptive physical education (APE) classes. Adaptive physical educators are specifically trained in adapting physical education instruction and activities for students with disabilities. Moreover, students with orthopedic impairments may need to be positioned throughout the school day. Physical therapists can provide valuable information about correct positions that the student may need.

APPLYING THE STRATEGIES

Deserre is included in the regular classroom for most of the school day. Ms. Bowden, her special education teacher, provides coteaching services in Deserre's general education math, social studies, science, and English language arts classes.

Various related service personnel routinely work with Deserre. She receives occupational therapy, physical therapy, speech and language services, and adaptive physical education in addition to the regular academic program. Deserre has enough functioning in her right hand so that she can operate the joystick to move her motorized wheelchair. Deserre requires head restraints in her wheelchair as she lacks the ability to hold her head in an upright position. She requires assistance with eating and uses adaptive eating utensils to feed herself. A female paraprofessional assists Deserre with her personal hygiene needs.

The strategies that follow are based on Deserre, who has cerebral palsy, and her teacher's desire to adapt the learning environment for her. Because orthopedic impairments vary, teachers need to learn as much as possible about the specific type of impairment in order to individualize the environment accordingly.

Working With the Whole Class

Some specific strategies for working with children with orthopedic impairments follow:

- *Ensure accessibility.* Mrs. Bowden found that many of the classrooms that Deserre would be in were difficult to negotiate. Together with Deserre's general education teachers, they rearranged furniture so that Deserre could easily move her wheelchair from one place to another.

- *Make plans for bathroom use.* Make plans for bathroom use, especially for those children who need a specially equipped bathroom, such as Deserre. A paraprofessional assisted Deserre with bathroom needs, but Deserre had to exit the general education classroom to go to the special education classroom where the accessible bathroom was located.

- *Prepare the class.* Mrs. Bowden worked with Deserre's general education teachers in preparing their classes in advance of Deserre being included. Mrs. Bowden described Deserre's special needs, and they all discussed ways in which they could help support Deserre as an active participant in the learning environment.

- *Coordinate related services.* Due to the related service personnel schedules, Deserre received some of the related services during her general education classes and had to be pulled out to the special education classroom. However, many of the services were implemented within the inclusive classroom to reduce the loss of instructional times. Mrs. Bowden and the related service personnel worked closely with the general education teachers to help them understand the importance of these services.

Working With Individual Children

Mrs. Bowden and Deserre's general education teachers implemented the following strategies for Deserre:

- *Provide assistive technology.* In surveying the inclusive classrooms, Mrs. Bowden determined that the computer tables were not accessible to Deserre and that they were not equipped with the assistive technology software and hardware that Deserre needed. Mrs. Bowden consulted with the occupational therapist in identifying the assistive technology and accessible computer tables for Deserre.

- *Identify appropriate positioning.* Because Deserre needed to be positioned throughout the school day, Mrs. Bowden worked with the occupational and physical therapists on the specific positions that Deserre needed. These positions were individually selected to address Deserre's needs and with knowledge that they would be implemented within an inclusive environment. Mrs. Bowden received specific training in proper lifting and positioning from the OT and PT.

◻ *Promote independence.* Promoting independence is important. The child should be allowed to maneuver herself as much as possible and to ask for help when needed. In the case of Deserre, mealtimes were particularly important in promoting independence. Deserre used adaptive utensils and could feed herself with some assistance. Knowing that it would take Deserre much longer to eat than her peers, Mrs. Bowden consulted the principal and was able to schedule a longer lunch period for Deserre.

◻ *Allow for response time.* Deserre required more time to respond to the teacher's requests than her typically developing peers. Mrs. Bowden and the general education teachers worked together to provide Deserre with adequate response time.

◻ *Provide adaptive physical education.* Deserre's IEP stipulated that she participate in adaptive physical education classes. The adaptive physical educator, Mr. Robinson, designed specific activities for Deserre and worked very closely with Deserre's physical therapist on the stretches, positioning, and movement that Deserre needed.

Working With Families:

Mrs. Bowden and Deserre's mother worked very closely with each other. Mrs. Bowden sent home a daily communication log and noted any special circumstances that occurred during the day. Because Deserre was often tired at the end of the school day, the communication log was critical in letting Deserre's mother know what happened during the day. Likewise, Deserre's mother notified Mrs. Bowden when there were changes in medicine and any special occurrences at home. Of particular note was when Deserre's wheelchair malfunctioned. Deserre's mother worked very closely with Mrs. Bowden and the occupational and physical therapists in providing an alternative motorized wheelchair while Deserre's was being repaired.

IF YOU WANT TO KNOW MORE

Physical Disabilities: The Special Ed Wiki—http://sped.wikidot.com/physical-disabilities

Physical Disabilities—http://specialed.about.com/od/physicaldisabilities/Physical_Disabilities.htm

Teaching and Orthopedic Impairment Students, Bright Hub—http://www.brighthub.com/education/special/articles/71197.aspx

Division for Physical, Health, and Multiple Disabilities—http://web.utk.edu/~dphmd

11

Hector

A STUDENT WITH INTELLECTUAL DISABILITIES

As Hector enters the first-grade classroom, he waves and says a loud "Hello!" to Ms. Jesse. Although Ms. Jesse is in the middle of teaching a small group of students, Hector does not seem to notice. He says hello again until Ms. Jesse looks in his direction. Ms. Jesse attended Hector's IEP meeting and is aware that Hector was recently diagnosed with an intellectual disability in the mild range of functioning. A few moments later, Mr. Reed, Hector's special education teacher, enters the room; he speaks softly to Hector and directs him to his desk. Once at his desk, Hector begins to look at a book on animals and starts singing "Old McDonald." Mr. Reed redirects Hector to "read" softly until Ms. Jesse is finished with her group of students.

OVERVIEW OF INTELLECTUAL DISABILITIES

What Are Intellectual Disabilities?

A student with an intellectual disability typically has significant limitations both in intellectual functioning (reasoning, problem solving, and learning) and in adaptive behavior (type of behavior exhibited in different social situations). This disability originates before the age of 18. These limitations in functioning will cause a child to learn and develop more slowly than a typical child.

According to the American Association of Intellectual and Developmental Disabilities (AAIDD, 2013), an intellectual disability (formerly termed mental retardation) is defined using the following three criteria:

1. Intellectual functioning level (IQ) is below 70–75;
2. Significant limitations exist in two or more adaptive skill areas (those skills needed to live, work, and play); and
3. The condition manifests itself before the age of 18.

The AAIDD definition includes 10 adaptive skills: communication, self-care, home living, social skills, leisure, health and safety, self-direction, functional academics, community use, and work. The Special Olympics (2008) clarified this further, noting that these skills are present across all aspect's of one's life and situated in one's personal environment. A child can have limits in his intellectual functioning but may not be diagnosed with an intellectual disability if he does not have limits in these adaptive skills.

These students may take longer to learn to walk, speak, and take care of their personal needs, such as dressing or eating, and thus may be functioning behind their same-aged classmates. They are also very likely to have trouble learning in school. They may take longer to learn some things, and they just may not learn others.

What Teachers Need to Know About Intellectual Disabilities

Just like any student with a disability, students with intellectual disabilities require that special education and related services be made available free of charge until age 21. These services should be specially designed to address the child's individual needs associated with the disability. School staff should collaborate with the child's parents to develop an IEP.

We strongly support the belief that students with intellectual disabilities be in the general education classroom. In addition, these students should be making progress with the same curriculum taught to those without disabilities. For that to happen, the teacher may need to make accommodations or modifications to the general education curriculum. Accommodations are reasonable adjustments to the curriculum for the student to be successful. These include audiobooks, typing homework assignments, and sitting at the front of the room. Modifications include changing or making the material easier (e.g., simplified or shorter assignments). If a student has a severe intellectual disability, the multidisciplinary team may also consider an alternative curriculum. This curriculum may focus more on life skills and be taught in a different setting.

Students will also be lacking in their adaptive skills, which are skills needed to live, work, and play in the community. Because these are important skills needed to function in society, teachers and parents can help a child work on these skills at both school and home. Some of these skills include (a) communicating with others; (b) health and safety; (c) reading, writing, and basic math; (d) taking care of personal needs (dressing, bathing, toileting); and (e) home living (helping to set the table, cleaning the house, or cooking dinner).

INCLUSIVE CLASSROOM STRATEGIES

Family Interventions

Families of children with intellectual disabilities may not be aware that their child has an intellectual disability until he or she is diagnosed in elementary school. Such is the case for children who have mild intellectual disabilities and are more likely to be diagnosed during the early school years. Once diagnosed, families will need support and assistance in understanding their child's unique strengths and weaknesses.

Classroom Interventions

Children who have intellectual disabilities (ID) and are in inclusive classroom settings bring with them a unique set of skills. As more and more children are being included in the general education setting, teachers must develop a wide range of instructional practices to meet the needs of all children. The following classroom interventions apply for children who have intellectual disabilities in the mild range of functioning and are in inclusive settings.

Reading. Generally, students with intellectual disabilities require repeated and explicit skill instruction. A student with an intellectual quotient (IQ) score of 70 will begin to acquire the skills of beginning reading at the end of the second grade. However, children with intellectual disabilities begin to read with comprehension even later. Thus, more language/study of word meaning and repeated practice is required (L. Kinnison, personal communication, August 7, 2012). This instruction must be paired with concrete examples that are relevant to the child's experiences and cognitive abilities. Explicit instruction is teacher-centered, direct instruction "where the teacher decides what to teach, the objectives are clear, and students are explicitly taught concepts and skills" (Hollingsworth & Ybarra, 2009, p. 10).

With respect to teaching children with ID to read, instructional practices should center on explicit, systematic instruction that is comprehensive and includes extensive cumulative review. Further, children should be taught precisely how to apply strategies in the context of reading connected text (Allor, Mathes, Champlin, & Cheatham, 2009). For children with ID, a comprehensive reading program includes (Allor et al., 2009):

- systematic, explicit instruction in all components of reading,
- repetitive, routine activities implemented with consistent instructional language, and
- fast-paced, short activities that are highly motivating (p. 12).

To implement effective reading programs, educators need to model skills and teach children how to apply skills learned in new situations. Further, immediate feedback and scaffolding of skills that are provided in motivating environments are critical to long-term success (Allor, Mathes, Jones, Champlin, & Cheatham, 2010).

Math. In the area of math, students with intellectual disabilities need to learn to responsibly manage personal finance, including counting money, making change, keeping financial records, calculating and paying taxes, and making purchases with credit cards or checks. Students also need to perform simple measurement calculations in order to prepare food and take care of a home.

In 2003, Kroesbergen and Van Luit completed a review of studies on mathematic interventions for elementary students with mild intellectual disabilities. Fifty-eight studies were investigated. Thirty-one out of the fifty-eight studies examined included basic fact strategies. The studies were analyzed using a random effects model by dividing the studies into three domains: preparatory arithmetic, acquisition and automaticity of basic math skills, and problem solving. Results indicated that most interventions studied in the meta-analysis addressed basic skills and that these interventions were the most effective. In studies focusing on problem solving, interventions for students with mild mental retardation were more effective than those for students with learning disabilities. Perhaps unexpectedly, interventions implemented over a longer time period were not as effective as those of shorter duration. Overall, self-instruction was most effective; however, direct instruction was most effective for specifically learning basic skills. In general, traditional interventions with teachers delivering the instruction (as opposed to computers) were most effective and mediated/assisted instruction was found to be less effective than either direct instruction or self-instruction. Lastly, interventions making use of peer tutoring were found to be less effective than other interventions.

Daily living. In addition to academic instruction, children with ID may require explicit instruction in the area of daily living (i.e., functional life skills). Daily living skills facilitate a person's ability to live, work, and be involved in recreational activities in the community environment (Mechling, Gast, & Langone, 2002). Functional curriculum may include communication, community living, domestic skills, socialization, self-help, and vocational and leisure skills (Mastropieri & Scruggs, 2010).

An example of a specific life skill that children with ID require explicit instruction in is the ability to purchase items. To purchase items, children must understand money management, how to locate items on the store shelves by reading signs, how to determine which item they wish to purchase among the many types of items available, how to identify the cost of the item, and how to pay for the purchase with the correct dollar amount (Mechling et al., 2002).

Peer Relationships

The interactions that children have with their peers play a central role in relationships, quality of life, and success in school. Thus, it is important that children with ID learn skills that enhance peer relationships in and out of school. Carter, Sisco, Chung, and Stanton-Chapman (2010) analyzed the following student-focused, peer interaction strategies for children with ID:

- *Augmentative and alternative communication (AAC) use:* Introducing AAC systems (e.g., pictures, communication books, and electronic systems) to students with disabilities and/or providing additional training to students; peers may or may not also receive training.
- *Cognitive-behavioral-ecological social skills training:* A training package consisting of (a) instruction in prerequisite social concepts, (b) affective education related to four basic emotions, and (c) social interpersonal problem solving.
- *Collateral skills:* Teaching students with disabilities other skills (e.g., game playing and computer skills) that are not explicitly social to enhance participation in leisure or other activities.
- *Conversational turn-taking:* Providing systematic instruction and conversational structures to facilitate balanced turn-taking by both partners in conversations.
- *Pivotal response training:* Naturalistic strategies designed to promote generalization by using multiple exemplars and incorporating a target student's preferences.
- *Self-management:* Teaching students with disabilities to self-manage their own social behaviors using goal setting, self-prompting, self-monitoring, self-evaluation, and related strategies.

    ❑   *Social stories:* Individualized stories that describe a specific social situation a student with disabilities may find challenging, explain the reactions of others to the situation, and provide examples of appropriate social responses.

    ❑   *Social skills:* Teaching students with disabilities general social and communication skills (not addressed in the other practices described above). (p. 68)

Transition Planning

It is never too early to begin the process of transition planning for students with disabilities. This planning is especially critical for students who have intellectual disabilities and may need assistance with life as an adult once they exit public education services. At the elementary level, it is vital that families contact state agencies that are responsible for assisting individuals with intellectual disabilities once they leave public education. Often these agencies have multiple-year waiting lists for services such as supported living programs or job coaching.

Planning for life after high school can often be an overwhelming and confusing process. The adoption of person-family approaches can help with the transition process. Person-family approaches emphasize the perspectives of persons with disabilities and their families. Further, planning should consider the choices of individuals with intellectual disabilities to the greatest degree possible (Kim & Turnbull, 2004).

APPLYING THE STRATEGIES

Mr. Reed, Hector's special education teacher, enters the room; he speaks softly to Hector and directs him to his desk. Once at his desk, Hector begins to look at a book on animals and starts singing "Old McDonald." Mr. Reed redirects Hector to "read" softly until Ms. Jesse is finished with her group of students.

Working With the Whole Class

After attending Hector's IEP meeting, Ms. Jesse consulted with Mr. Reed about inclusive strategies that they might try in her classroom to assist Hector in meeting his IEP goals and objectives.

    ❑   *Provide explicit instruction.* When teaching lessons, Ms. Jesse used explicit instruction. For example, when teaching reading, Ms. Jesse used the strategy Point and Read. In this strategy, simple sentences related to the storybook that was being read aloud were printed in large text with pictures. The teacher reads the sentence to the children, pointing as each word is read. Then the children repeat the sentence as they point to each word (Allor et al., 2009).

☐ *Incorporate social skills:* Because social skills are important for all first graders, Ms. Jesse and Mr. Reed embedded social skills lessons throughout the school day (e.g., turn taking, sharing during center time, listening to stories, saying please and thank you).

☐ *Provide concrete examples.* Many students in first grade need models and concrete examples to connect prior knowledge to new knowledge that is being taught. Ms. Jesse provided concrete examples throughout her lessons (e.g., manipulatives, counting blocks, magnetic letters, etc.).

☐ *Coteach:* Mr. Reed cotaught with Ms. Jesse in the inclusive setting to help Hector navigate the general education classroom. According to coteaching practices, Mr. Reed and Ms. Jesse collaboratively planned lessons and switched roles. Sometimes Mr. Reed would lead the whole-group lessons while Ms. Jesse worked with small groups. Conversely, Ms. Jesse would lead whole-group lessons, and Mr. Reed would work individually with students or with small groups. In this way, Mr. Reed and Ms. Jesse shared the responsibility of teaching all students in the classroom.

Working With Individual Children

Ms. Jesse consulted with Mr. Reed about Hector's IEP before Hector's first day in Ms. Jesse's inclusive classroom. Together, they worked on activities and lessons that would specifically address Hector's special needs within the inclusive setting. The following are specific interventions that they implemented:

☐ *Provide explicit instruction.* Hector required systematic, explicit instruction in all areas: reading, math, daily living, and peer interactions. For example, Ms. Jesse and Mr. Reed used Point and Read with Hector in a small-group setting of 3–4 students to help develop his oral language skills and concepts of print.

☐ *Provide picture cues.* Because Hector was an emergent reader, Mr. Reed and Ms. Jesse posted a picture schedule on Hector's desk. In addition, they paired classroom posters, rules, and classroom activities with picture cues.

☐ *Provide concrete examples.* Ms. Jesse knew that Hector needed concrete examples that were relevant to his experiences. She and Mr. Reed supplemented instruction and learning centers with objects they collected from home and from the community.

☐ *Pair with a peer buddy.* Mr. Reed and Ms. Jesse paired Hector with a typically-developing peer buddy who assisted Hector with transitions in the classroom, activities and lessons, and who could help Hector develop his peer interactions and social skills in a supportive environment.

◻ *Create social stories.* Mr. Reed and Ms. Jesse created social stories for Hector that focused on peer interactions and social skills that Hector found challenging. Mr. Reed and Ms. Jesse would read the social stories individually with Hector and send them home in Hector's backpack for his family to read to him in the evening and on weekends.

◻ *Offer one-step directions.* When giving directions, Mr. Reed and Ms. Jesse gave Hector one-step instructions. When they observed that Hector completed the first task, they would give him the second step to complete, and so on.

Working With Families

Mr. Reed understood that Hector's family was having a difficult time with accepting the diagnosis that Hector was a child with an intellectual disability. He knew that they needed time to grieve and come to terms with the diagnosis. Mr. Reed facilitated this process by implementing the following strategies:

◻ *Provide agency information.* Mr. Reed knew that to receive services for Hector when he exited public school, Hector's family needed to take action now, as there were long waiting lists for these services. Mr. Reed provided Hector's family with contact information for the appropriate state agencies so that they could start planning for Hector's future now.

◻ *Refer to counseling.* Mr. Reed referred Hector's family to the school counselor who could assist Hector's family in obtaining counseling services.

◻ *Create a communication log.* Mr. Reed and Ms. Jesse documented Hector's activities and progress toward his goals and objectives in a daily communication log that they sent home in Hector's backpack.

◻ *Create social stories.* Mr. Reed and Ms. Jesse worked with Hector's family to create social stories for situations that occurred at home. They reviewed the stories with Hector during the school day to help reinforce the information and facilitate generalization of skills.

IF YOU WANT TO KNOW MORE

The Division on Autism and Developmental Disabilities—http://daddcec.org/Home.aspx

Intellectual Disability, National Dissemination Center for Children with Disabilities—http://nichcy.org/disability/specific/intellectual

Center for Disease Control and Prevention: Intellectual Disability Fact Sheet—http://www.cdc.gov/ncbddd/actearly/pdf/parents_pdfs/IntellectualDisability.pdf

12

Technology for Students With Disabilities

Over the years, technology has gone from nonexistent in classrooms or not impacting instruction to being in almost every classroom and a major part of the instructional process. Teachers use technology, students use technology, and teacher preparation programs prepare future teachers to incorporate technology into the instructional process. Technology is changing the way teachers do their work and opening up more opportunities for teachers and students.

Technology alone, however, will not revolutionize education. It can and probably will impact education like no other innovation we have experienced: "Any technology, whether it be personal computers or specific technology designed for particular populations (i.e., augmentative and alternative communication devices, and text-to-speech), will not radically transform education" (Bouck, 2010). After all, technology is a tool (Edyburn, 2001). Technology in the classroom is just one tool used to assist teachers in educating students in academic, social, or functional skills.

TECHNOLOGY: A HUGE POSSIBILITY

Technology is perceived as a means of providing access and opportunity, promoting independence, and encouraging empowerment for students with disabilities (Edyburn, Higgins, & Boone, 2005). Technology has the capability of benefitting students with disabilities and solving many of the challenges they face. Technology can give students with disabilities access to opportunities and/ or experiences previously not afforded them. Technology can be a powerful tool to help students be successful in the elementary classroom. Technology can be a voice for students who may not have one because of their disability (e.g., AAC devices), read a text out loud to a student who learns through listening and has trouble comprehending written text (e.g., text-to-speech devices, screen readers, and Reading Pens), help students organize their day (with the use of a calendar), and provide access to important tools (e.g., switches and speech recognition), to name just a few things. Technology is definitely not the absolute solution to every problem, but it is an area that all elementary school teachers should consider.

Teachers can incorporate technology into their instruction to make presentations more coherent, realistic, and exciting. It can also be used to supplement instruction. Access to the Internet allows teachers to show students experiments, explain with specific examples, and search for unknown answers. It allows teachers to demonstrate to students how to be good consumers of information on the Internet, how to decide if information is truthful or not, and what sites are appropriate or not. Not only is technology capable of helping teachers, but it can be beneficial to students.

THE LEGAL ASPECTS OF ASSISTIVE TECHNOLOGY

Assistive technology, which refers to both devices and services, represents an important consideration for students with disabilities. The definition of assistive technology devices and services stem from the 1988 Technology-Related Assistance for Individuals with Disabilities Act (P.L. 100-407), typically referred to as the Tech Act. An assistive technology device, defined as "any item, piece of equipment, or product system, whether acquired commercially off the shelf, modified, or customized, that is used to increase, maintain, or improve the functional capabilities of a child with a disability," is a related service to be considered for students with disabilities as part of their IEP (IDEA, 2004, Section 300.5). An assistive technology service, which sometimes is overlooked because it isn't a "piece" of equipment (Parette, Peterson-Karlan, & Wojcik, 2005), is defined as "any service that directly assists an individual in the selection, acquisition, or use of an assistive technology device" (Tech Act, 1988). This means that assistive technology can either be a tool (e.g., graph paper) or a service (e.g., training for the student on the use of some sort of assistive technology) that supports students in acquiring or using assistive technology.

ASSISTIVE TECHNOLOGY AND STUDENTS WITH DISABILITIES

Assistive technology is an important consideration for all students with disabilities. Assistive technology for students with low-incidence or severe disabilities may look different than assistive technology for students with high-incidence disabilities (Smith, 2010). For both groups, assistive technology improves the academic and life functioning of these students and improves their quality of life (Edyburn et al., 2005).

Assistive Technology Considerations

The IEP team is responsible for making decisions regarding assistive technology for students with disabilities. The decision-making process of choosing assistive technology is a monumental responsibility when one considers the power of assistive technology. For example, assistive technology is just one way to provide access and opportunity, promote independence, and encourage the empowerment of students with disabilities (Edyburn et al., 2005). In other words, technology can compensate for a student's challenges or disability and allow them to be more, if not fully, functional in the classroom and/or society.

Assistive technology can help students with disabilities gain better access to the general education environment as well as curriculum (Christ, 2008). Much research has documented the overall benefits of assistive technology for all students and particularly assistive technology for students with high-incidence disabilities (Edyburn, 2000; Edyburn et al., 2005; Lahm, 2003; Quinn et al., 2009). But when it comes to assistive technology, there are many different options.

TYPES OF TECHNOLOGY

The definition of assistive technology is very open to interpretation, and thus it allows for a continuum of assistive technology, which is typically conceptualized by the level of technology. Depending on the model, the assistive technology continuum can be low-tech and high-tech; no tech, low-tech, and high-tech; or low-tech, moderate-tech, and high-tech (Blackhurst, 1997; Edyburn, 2005;

Johnson, Beard, & Carpenter, 2007; Vanderheiden, 1984). Although the terms can be interpreted differently, most professionals understand no-tech assistive technology to be a tool or support that requires no technology (e.g., a mnemonic strategy; Behrmann & Jerome, 2002). Low-tech assistive technology is then, typically, a tool or device that requires very little technology and is usually lower in cost (e.g., graph paper; Behrmann & Schaff, 2001). Moderate-tech assistive technology would require more technology. It might involve the use of batteries but would not be computer-based and would cost more than low-tech assistive technology (e.g., a calculator). Finally, high-tech assistive technology tends to be the most expensive devices and tools and are generally computer-based (e.g., text-to-speech; Edyburn, 2005; Johnson et al., 2007; Vanderheiden, 1984). Although a device's categorization is not important, what is important is knowing that assistive technology exists on a continuum. Educators should be aware that low-tech options exist for consideration as assistive technology solutions for students with disabilities, and, in fact, the low-tech end of the continuum is where teachers should begin their investigations into appropriate tools to meet the challenges students face.

Along with the continuum of technology, devices are often categorized by the task for which they will provide compensation (Gierach, 2009). This list is by no means exhaustive, but common categories include the following:

- the motor aspects of writing, such as holding a writing utensil (e.g., pencil grips);
- composing written expression, such as ability to organize thoughts on paper (e.g., graphic organizers);
- computer access (e.g., touch screen);
- reading (e.g., text-to-speech, highlighter strips);
- communication (e.g., augmentative and alternative communication, such as Picture Exchange Communication Systems, Dynvox, sign language);
- mathematics (e.g., calculators, manipulatives);
- daily living tasks (e.g., weighted utensils, talking microwaves);
- mobility (e.g., gait trainer, wheelchair);
- vision (e.g., Braille or large print materials); and
- hearing (e.g., hearing aids).

The continuum of technology devices exists within each of these categories. For example, although a pencil grip is a low-tech assistive technology for motor aspects of writing, a portable keyboard (e.g., the Writer Plus or the Neo) could be considered a high-tech assistive technology tool for the same category.

CATEGORIZATION OF ASSISTIVE TECHNOLOGY

Within the broad and relatively ambiguous definition of assistive technology (e.g., "any items, product system . . . ") is some semblance of clarity through categorization. In other words, there are different categories through which to understand assistive technology. The first type of categorization is by level of technology, which was just discussed.

Assistive technology can also be categorized by type or purpose, of which there are seven: positioning, mobility, augmentative and alternative communication, computer access, adaptive toys and games, adaptive environments, and instructional aids (Bryant & Bryant, 2003). Most relevant to students with disabilities is assistive technology that targets instruction or learning within the key academic areas of reading, writing, and mathematics.

Reading

Two-thirds of students with learning disabilities read two to three grade levels below their peers without a learning disability, and a quarter of these students are reading more than five grade levels behind their peers (Wagner et al., 2003). Nearly 80% of students with a learning disability receive some type of service in the academic area of reading (Bryant, Young, & Dickson, 2001), and these students often struggle with gaining information through traditional print. As students progress through elementary school, the emphasis on the act of reading shifts from learning how to read to reading to learn (Mason & Hedin, 2011). In other words, as students get older, classroom reading instruction changes from teaching basic reading skills to teaching subject content (e.g., history or economics). Often teaching content is done with textbooks, and students are expected to use basic reading skills to learn about the content area. When a student struggles with reading, the task of reading to learn becomes an insurmountable barrier to learning. In addition, textbooks often have a text structure that is "inconsiderate" or awkward, filled with factual information, lacking in predictability (Bakken, Mastropieri, & Scruggs, 1997; Gillam, Fargo, & Robertson, 2009), and often poorly written, which makes comprehension difficult for students.

Challenges with reading can have detrimental outcomes. Students with mild disabilities are more likely to drop out of high school compared to students who do not have a learning disability (nearly 33% vs. 11%; U.S. Department of Education, 2003). Not being able to read and read well affects students with disabilities beyond dropping out of high school; they are less likely to attend postsecondary schools, have a higher attrition rate when they do attend postsecondary schools, and are less likely to experience career success (Burgstahler, 2003).

However, there are a variety of assistive technology options to decrease or remove barriers that traditional print creates for students with disabilities.

- ◻ *Text-to-speech.* Text-to-speech software provides computer-synthesized speech to read digital text to students (Courtad, 2011). Text-to-speech software allows students to hear and read a text selection (i.e., words are highlighted as the software speaks them). Many text-to-speech programs allow for customization to meet students' needs or desires (e.g., the number of words read per minute, rate, voice). Text-to-speech is a versatile assistive technology; it can be used on computers, personal computing devices, handheld devices (i.e., iPad, iTouch, Netbook), or eReaders (i.e., Kindle, Nook, iPad). The best part is that this software can currently be acquired for free (e.g., Natural Reader, Read Please).

- ◻ *Accessible text.* Accessible text is text that can be either transformed or manipulated into another format other than traditional print (Stahl, 2004); accessible text is commonly called digital text or eText for students with disabilities (Boone & Higgins, 2007). Due in part to the mandate for accessible materials and the availability of computers and eReaders, this technology for students with disabilities has experienced a rapid increase (Stahl, 2004). In addition to using accessible text with personal devices, software allows digital text to be imported into mp3 files and read aloud on such players as an iPod. Accessible text allows students to access material above their current reading level.

- ◻ *Supported eText.* Supported eText is digital or electronic text supplemented with rewording, description, media, highlighted text, or other strategies to increase comprehension of material (Anderson-Inman, 2009; Anderson-Inman & Horney, 2007). Use of supported eText has an emerging research base (Anderson-Inman, 2009): Existing literature found supported eText improved the reading comprehension achievement of high school students with mild to moderate disabilities (Izzo, Yurick, & McArrell, 2009), and, in some cases, aided in comprehension related to functional skills for students with intellectual disabilities (Douglas, Ayres, Langone, Bell, & Meade, 2009).

Writing

Another academic area students with mild disabilities often have deficits in is that of writing. These students often write at a slower pace, have frequent misspellings, and lack basic grammar and sentence structure (MacArthur, 2009). Students who lack these skills experience a disadvantage in classrooms. They often do not write what they know, nor do they extend their knowledge with writing, and subsequently their grades suffer (MacArthur, 2009). Beyond grades, students with a deficit in written language can encounter problems in the adult world, as writing becomes integrated in daily work life. E-mail is frequently used in the workplace and other written communication is required in the business world as a way to communicate knowledge, orders, or descriptions. If an individual cannot communicate through writing, he will be at a disadvantage throughout life. Fortunately, there are commonplace tools that can support a person's writing without intrusion (MacArthur, 2006).

- *Word processing.* The word processor has proven to be a powerful tool during the writing process for those with and without disabilities (MacArthur, 2009). Word processing programs are readily available in schools and support the recursive nature of writing, or, in other words, that writing pieces should be revisited, revised, added to, and edited during the writing process (MacArthur, 2009). The use of a word processor can make the writing process (from ideas, to writing, to editing, to revising) easier for students, and it also allows them to function more like their classmates. Students are also able to save their work and come back and either finish it or edit it at a later time. There is no need for students to rush through their writing task, as they will always have access to it.

  In addition to helping students with the writing process, word processors can help students with mild disabilities who also have handwriting difficulties. Handwriting needs to be legible so the message can be read by the student and others, and handwriting must also be fluent so as not to interrupt the writing process (MacArthur, 2009). Students with disabilities often have very sloppy writing that is hard for the teacher and themselves to read. In addition to written products, a word processor or computer could also be used for note-taking in other academic classes. Hetzroni and Shrieber (2004) found word processors for junior high students with LD increased their writing performance in the areas of spelling, number of words written, and their ability to produce legible text when compared to paper-pencil writings. The ability to type text can remove many of the physical fine motor barriers involved in traditional pencil and paper transcribing. There are also different types of keyboards available that can be smaller or larger than the normal size to aid students during this process. It is best if the teacher works with the student to find the best possible alternative to help them be successful.

- *Spell checkers.* Similar to using word processing for writing, spell checkers can be an integral part of classrooms (Peterson-Karlan, 2011). The majority of word processing programs, as well as most e-mail software programs, blog posts, and smartphones, have embedded spell checkers. Spell checkers can aid the student with disabilities during the drafting process and increase fluency and confidence (Montgomery & Marks,

2006). Students are free to work on getting their thoughts down on the computer without having to worry about the exact spelling of each word. When paired with other assistive technologies (e.g., text-to-speech technology), spell checkers can increase a student's independence during the editing stage (Montgomery & Marks, 2006).

◻ *Graphic organizers and planning tools.* Struggling writers often skip important steps in the writing process. These steps include planning, revising, and editing. When students are directly taught specific strategies, they are more likely to be successful during the writing process. Paper, software, or online graphic organizers aid in the planning and revision of written content (Santangelo & Olinghouse, 2009) and allow students to visually represent their ideas or text structure. Blair, Ormsbee, & Brandes (2002) studied graphic organizer software use with 24 seventh- and eighth-grade students with mild disabilities. Although the duration of the intervention was short, students consistently and effectively used graphic organizer software (i.e., Inspiration) to plan and organize their writing, presented a more positive attitude to writing, and produced longer and higher quality writing pieces.

Mathematics

Technology to support mathematics for students with disabilities includes not only that which can support access to the mathematics (e.g., literacy tools) but also tools to support both computation as well as problem-solving. Research-supported, mathematics-specific technologies for students with disabilities include the calculator (e.g., four-function, scientific, or graphing), manipulatives, and computer-assisted instruction (Bouck & Flanagan, 2009). Although research on calculator use for students with disabilities is limited—most is focused on calculators as an accommodation for assessments—the little literature on students with high-incidence disabilities in general is supportive of calculator use (Bethell & Miller, 1998; Bouck, Joshi, & Johnson, in press). For example, Bouck et al. (in press) found students with and without disabilities who used calculators on multiple-choice and open-ended problems were more likely to answer questions correctly. Calculators can help students with the factual information to process answers. For example, a student might have a difficult time remembering her basic multiplication facts and thus gets all of her problems wrong, even though she understands the process of how to get the correct answer to a problem. The calculator then helps the student with the facts so that she can process the information correctly. There is also a very strong research base from the field of general education to support calculator use with students, such as improved conceptual understanding, improved problem-solving skills, and no negative consequences associated with skill development (Ellington, 2003). In addition, calculators can also lighten the cognitive load for students with disabilities (Sharma & Hannafin, 2007).

Concrete manipulatives also have a strong literature base for their use with students with and without disabilities (Huntington, 1995). The use of concrete manipulatives is actually considered a best practice for mathematics education of secondary students with disabilities (Maccini & Gagnon, 2000). Researchers found that the use of concrete manipulatives resulted in students successfully solving mathematics word problems (e.g., a geoboard for solving area and perimeter problems or Cuisenaire rods for learning correct operations) more accurately (Cass, Cates, Smith, & Jackson, 2003). The good news is that teachers with a low budget can use typical household objects for manipulatives (e.g., popsicle sticks and cotton balls). Concrete manipulatives can support students in learning through a hands-on, concrete experience and can assist students with disabilities in developing conceptual understanding through progressing from concrete (i.e., physical, concrete manipulative, such as tiles or fraction strips) to semiconcrete (i.e., pictorial representations) to abstract (i.e., symbols, such as numbers and operations), known as the concrete-semiconcrete-abstract (CSA) approach (Jordan, Miller, & Mercer, 1998).

Beyond concrete manipulatives, teachers might consider using virtual manipulatives, which are typically virtual replicas of the concrete objects or, in other words, interactive online tools (Reimer & Moyer, 2005). Although minimal research exists on virtual manipulatives to support students with disabilities in mathematics, this technology remains an option, particularly for teachers who may have limited access to concrete manipulatives (see Bouck & Flanagan, 2010, for a detailed discussion of different websites for virtual manipulatives and examples of how to implement them in practice). The research on virtual manipulatives for students in general is positive in terms of student learning, as well as student motivation (Reimer & Moyer, 2005; Steen, Brooks, & Lyon, 2006).

Computer-assisted instruction (CAI) is another popular support for students with disabilities in mathematics. CAI is defined as "computer programs that provide drill-and-practice, tutorial, or simulation activities offered either by themselves or as supplements to traditional, teacher-directed instruction" (Cotton, 1991, p. 2). Although researchers studying students with high-incidence disabilities found CAI offered benefits to students in terms of computation and problem-solving (e.g., Seo & Bryant, 2010), a recent meta-analysis by Seo and Bryant (2009) exploring CAI and mathematics with students with disabilities reported the effectiveness of CAI for mathematics performance was inconclusive from the 11 studies they reviewed between 1980 and 2008. However, it should be noted that the studies reviewed had methodological flaws that may have contributed to the results and they primarily focused on elementary-aged students and basic facts (e.g., addition or multiplication; Seo & Bryant, 2009, 2010).

ORGANIZATION AND SELF-MANAGEMENT

Assistive technology can also help students with disabilities in other areas in and after school experiences. In fact, teachers rate organizational behaviors (e.g., being prepared for class, making deadlines, following directions, and neatness and organization) as beneficial to academic outcomes (McMullen, Shippen, & Dangel, 2007) and important to students if they want to be successful. Common technology that makes life easier for individuals can act as assistive technology for students with mild disabilities in terms of executive functioning (Bouck et al., 2012; Johnson et al., 2007). For example, students with mild disabilities can use smartphones, smartpens (e.g., Livescribe™—the Pulse and Echo), personal digital assistants, and handheld devices (e.g., iPod or iPad) to assist them with organization and memory tasks (Johnson et al., 2007; LoPresti, Mihailidis, & Kirsch, 2004). These handheld, portable devices can provide accessibility as well as support students who struggle with organization and memory (e.g., note-taking with audio recording, reminders—visual and auditory, calendar features, and to-do lists; Shrieber & Seifert, 2009). Livescribe™ smartpens are very innovative as they operate like regular pens, but they also have built-in microphones and cameras to record what students are writing as well as the actual dialogue taking place (e.g., a conversation with a teacher).

Other technology can be used to actively teach students with mild disabilities self-management skills. Fitzgerald and colleagues developed the KidTool Support System™ (KTSS), an electronic performance support system designed to target behavior and academic performance of students with high-incidence disabilities (Mitchem, Kight, Fitzgerald, & Koury, 2007). Programs within the KTSS support and teach students regulation, problem-solving, organization, and learning strategies (Fitzgerald & Koury, 2001–2002, 2004–2005).

Increasingly, advanced forms of technology are being used for organizational purposes for students in schools, although the lower-tech form of datebooks and school planners still exist. Some schools have moved to all students using Netbooks for their school work. Students have access to assignments, lectures, and online textbooks for all of their classes. They can also use Netbooks for their homework and to work collaboratively with other students in their classes. Students use personal data managers to help them organize their calendars, as well as keep track of assignments, and there are more apps being developed daily that serve a personal or academic use to help the student be more successful (e.g., those for smartphones, iPads, or iPods). However, one stand-alone tool to support students with organization and memory is the WatchMinder, a sports watch that can be programmed to provide 30 alarms in addition to 65 preprogrammed messages for things like taking medication, staying on task, turning in an assignment, or studying for a test.

CONCLUSION

Overall, technology can benefit the elementary classroom teacher as well as the student with and without disabilities. Not only does assistive technology promote access, such as in a text-to-speech reader or eBook, but it also can improve students' success in the elementary classroom. Hence, assistive technology should always be a consideration for students with disabilities. Assistive technology holds promise to support students with disabilities in the core content areas (e.g., literacy, mathematics) as well as with other areas where students with disabilities seem to struggle, such as self-management and organization.

It is important to remember that technology is changing and will continue to change at a very rapid pace. Although it is not possible to predict where technology will go in the future, it is likely to continue down the path of greater portability and increased access for all students with disabilities. The future may also see technology (in general, as well as assistive technology) become more of an everyday occurrence in elementary classrooms. Instead of having to go through a process to get access to the needed technology, it will be a common commodity in elementary classrooms. Whatever the future holds, it will include technology, and technology will continue to provide support and level the playing field for students with disabilities in elementary classrooms.

CHAPTER 13

Collaborating With Families of Students in Inclusive Classrooms

Who knows a child any better and has been with the child longer than parents? From birth to school age and beyond, parents probably spend more time with their children than anyone else. Parents are involved with helping their children grow and develop and learn about what is socially acceptable, as well as learn some of the basic academic concepts. The value that parents are able to add to the learning experiences of their children cannot be duplicated. Likewise, their communication with teachers is essential when their children enroll in formal education. Support from parents will often help to create and/or strengthen school practices (Cook, Shepherd, Cook, & Cook, 2012). Historically, as well as currently, many parents have not participated a great deal in the planning, design, and implementation of their child's IEP (Martin, Marshall, & Sale, 2004). Because of the value associated with parental input, legal mandates have been put in place to ensure that parents of students with disabilities be included in the IEP process (IDEA, 2004). Collaboration with parents is essential to the success of their child, and the focus on parents has shifted from them as recipients of professional decisions to people who have valuable input in the decision-making process. Oftentimes, one roadblock to parental involvement is their knowledge level or perceived lack of knowledge regarding special education. Perhaps much of the hesitation to fully collaborating with parents is a naïve belief that educational professionals are more knowledgeable about the child and know how to address his or her academic deficits better than the parents. Teachers may know more about successful strategies to implement in the classroom, but parents could have valuable insight into their child's learning characteristics.

IDEA (2004) is known for safeguarding the provision of a free and appropriate public education for all students with disabilities. Regardless of the severity of the disability, all students have the right to an education. For some parents of children with disabilities who are beginning school, there is already a negative relationship and lack of collaboration between the school and parents. Teachers need to reach out to parents, communicate in many different ways with them (i.e., paper, e-mail, and phone), include them in decision making, and value their input. It is important that parents feel valued and are considered contributors in the educational process. Gordon and Miller (2003) conducted a study in an urban school district in which more than 200 school professionals and 80 parents participated in interviews to examine the self-efficacy of parents as contributing members to their child's IEP. According to the data collected, nearly 10 families were not even aware that their child was receiving special education services and approximately 30 families acknowledged their children's participation in a special education program but had little knowledge or understanding about their child's disability and the services their child was receiving. As the data pointed out, 45% of the families were not acquainted with their child's IEP and mandated services. This means they had no idea about the areas in which the child was deficient or what the school was doing to remediate these deficiencies. In addition, because they lacked specific knowledge, they could not reinforce needed skills at home. On the other hand, school professionals believed parents and families were knowledgeable about the IEP and felt that their school district was successful at facilitating collaboration with families (Gordon & Miller, 2003). Such inconsistencies in perceptions and reality contributed to ineffective collaboration and many different barriers. When mutual respect is achieved and open communication exists, parents and professionals benefit, and they can both grow and develop. Moreover, effective collaboration between families and professionals promotes a system in which both parties can work together to achieve shared goals for the student (Mueller, 2009). Effective collaboration with families and students with disabilities should continue throughout the year, not just during annual IEP meeting time. Collaboration should empower students with disabilities and their families and be strategically used to connect academic and social skills taught within the school.

Parent Types

Parents are involved in shaping individuals' early physical and emotional development. Just as there are different types of students and disabilities, there are different types of parents. Parents can be classified in general terms as *authoritative, authoritarian,* and *laissez-faire* (Baumrind, 1967). Other ways to classify different types of parents include terms such as *supportive, rejecting,* and *overinvolved.* Authoritarian and laissez-faire as well as rejecting and overinvolved parenting styles seem to heighten the behavior problems of children. Overinvolved parents (now known as "helicopter parents") cause problems for their children's teachers and school (Williams, 2008). Many times, these parents do not allow their children to live their own lives. They want to be involved in every aspect of their child's life and control what their child does and does not do, including grading, assignments, instruction, friends, and everything that happens in school.

It is, however, incorrect to suggest that all of the problems faced by individuals with disabilities are the result of their parents. In some cases, the characteristics of the individuals themselves are related to the way that parents interact with them, even as infants (Carey, 2009; Chess & Thomas, 1996). Temperament can enable a child to be more encouraging of interaction or more difficult to be around. The way a child responds to stimuli provided by the parents can have a positive or negative effect on them. This response can also impact how much a parent is involved in the child's overall development (academic and social). No one is prepared for being a parent, never mind a parent of a child with a disability. That is why it is so important that teachers reach out to parents, work with them, collaborate with them, and support them, letting them know that they are not alone in this lifelong process of education.

Parent Satisfaction With Services

Parents of individuals with disabilities frequently report that it is difficult to navigate the special education system. This common theme for parents is a very challenging aspect of special education. Navigating the general education system as well as the special education system is a daunting task for some parents and likely to be frustrating as well as confusing. The system of agencies, caseworkers, eligibility requirements, and funding restrictions can appear to be impenetrable.

Movement to inclusion and response to intervention (RtI) from "traditional" special education models further confounds the issue. Over time labels have changed, where students are to receive their education has changed (see Figure 13 for a diagram showing the many possible placements for students with special needs), and who is ultimately responsible for the child's learning has changed. The problem is that parents can have a hard time keeping up with all of the changes. It is the responsibility of the school and the teachers to thoroughly inform and

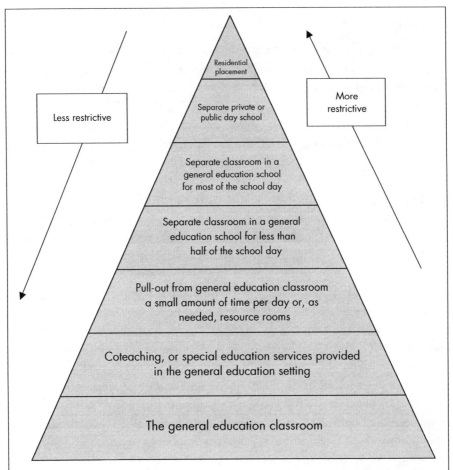

Figure 13. Continuum of special education placements. From *School Success for Kids With Emotional and Behavioral Disorders* (p. 193) by M. R. Davis, V. P. Culotta, E. A. Levine, and E. H. Rice, 2011, Waco, TX: Prufrock Press. Copyright 2011 Prufrock Press. Reprinted with permission.

educate parents of all the changes, and the only way this is going to happen is if the teachers and the parents have a well-established relationship.

PARENTS/FAMILY INVOLVEMENT

Not only must teachers consider parents of children with disabilities, but they also must consider if the family is from a culturally diverse background. Do teachers need to do things differently? What should teachers do to get culturally diverse families involved in the educational process of their children? Geenen, Powers, and Lopez-Vasquez (2001) indicated that educators are faced with many challenges in trying to increase the level and degree of involvement of parents from culturally diverse backgrounds. Parents from culturally diverse backgrounds are faced with a multitude of problems—such as language or cultural differences and, possibly, low-socioeconomic circumstances—that may interfere with their ability to be active participants and contributors in their child's education. Families who are in poverty expend a greater proportion of energy, time, and resources to meet their basic needs than do more privileged families, thus decreasing their abilities to adapt to and respond to the needs of their children with a disability.

Parents Who Are Culturally and Linguistically Diverse

Although culturally and linguistically diverse (CLD) parents sometimes know more than anyone else about their children, their insights and knowledge can oftentimes be devalued or ignored in the professional world by teachers, administrators, and support staff (Pena, 2000). As a result, many CLD families come to view the educational system as a bureaucracy controlled by educated, monocultural, monolingual individuals whom they have no power to question (Geenen et al., 2001; Neece, Kraemer, & Blacher, 2009). These parents view the school system as a negative institution where they have no value or input in any of the decision making regarding their child with a disability.

Trust is a critical aspect and absolutely necessary to create and sustain any successful relationship. Researchers have suggested that culturally and linguistically diverse families have a distinct mistrust toward formal American institutions because of historic and present-day discriminatory practices (Boyd & Correa, 2005; Harry, 2002; Obiakor, 2008). Overt and covert racism increases the likelihood that CLD students are singled out for special education and that their parents are falsely labeled as not caring about their education (Yawn, Hill, Obiakor, Gala, & Neu, 2013). Every situation should be treated individually, and all decisions should be unbiased and nonprejudiced toward the students with disabilities.

Teachers' lack of sensitivity to diversity might cause parents to feel disengaged from schools (Smith, Stern, & Shatrova, 2008), avoid participation in meetings, and communicate less effectively with others regarding school-related issues and their child with a disability. This lack of engagement and participation could have a detrimental effect on the student and his schooling. Additionally, CLD parents may perceive other barriers to collaboration, including (a) meetings at times that are inconvenient or not appropriate for them (Turney & Kao, 2009), (b) information about services and parents' rights presented through written materials in English higher than a fifth-grade reading level (families may have limited literacy skills or may be non-English speaking immigrants who are illiterate in their native language; Lareau, 2000), and (c) little effort on the part of professionals to seek families' input when making decisions about their child's education (Pena,

2000) or to learn about the culture of the student and the family involved in the collaboration.

Educators may view the parental responses as neglectful or ill-informed, but cultural perspectives of how parents understand and cope with their child's differences must be acknowledged. How the student actually becomes identified as needing special education and what that special programming may encompass is also very culture specific. The majority of assessment instruments and programming strategies have been historically developed and norm-referenced using data from Western countries and cultures (Rose & Huefner, 1984). In other words, most of these instruments and strategies have focused on White, middle-class individuals, so when a culturally different student is involved in this process, special attention needs to be taken when assessing and developing programs to ensure practices are equitable and fair. When educators discuss disability and how it is addressed culturally in the United States, they must remain sensitive and tolerant of parents' varied cultural perspectives and try to understand the disability from the perspective of the parents. Discussing the specific disability with the parents and getting their feelings and perspectives on it might go a long way toward improving communication in the future.

There are also other factors that can potentially decrease parental involvement. These factors include:

- inadequate or poor economic and cultural circumstances, which can increase communication and language barriers (Crosnoe, 2001; Lareau, 2000);
- lack of transportation to and from school and/or child care after school (Turney & Kao, 2009);
- lack of feeling welcome (Turney & Kao, 2009);
- cultural misinterpretation in help-seeking behavior (Smith et al., 2008);
- poor relationships with schools in the past (Cooper, 2009; Sturges, Cramer, Harry, & Klingner, 2005);
- negative beliefs about the student's disability (Green, 2009); and
- poor perceptions of professionals as experts (Gross, Julion, & Fogg, 2001).

Given all of these factors, it is apparent that teachers have their work cut out for them. Knowing the issues, however, is half the battle. Teachers can be proactive and approachable, as well as truly understanding of how these factors might impact the family and its participation or lack of participation with the teacher and/or school.

Parents with little education and limited English proficiency may find participation in school programs particularly difficult. As a result, some parents may assume a passive role in the educational decision-making process (Turnbull & Turnbull, 2000). Involving interpreters for non-English speaking families could be something that teachers and/or schools institute. Interpreters could help to breech the language barrier and communicate with the parents and family. This step would go a long way in showing parents that their participation and input is valued.

The issue of parental involvement must be faced directly. If successful education depends on parents actively working with the schools and if the parents do not become involved due to cultural differences, schools are faced with a major dilemma. Halpern (1992) concisely captured this conundrum:

> If our needed educational reform can only be accomplished with the assistance of parents, and if some parents want to abdicate this responsibility, and if policymakers are afraid or unwilling to confront the issue, many of the problems that currently bedevil the schools will remain unresolved. Students with disabilities, of course, will be caught up in the vortex of these unresolved problems, which must inevitably have an impact on opportunities that are available within special education and transition programs whether or not parents of students with disabilities are actively involved in these programs. (pp. 210–211)

Parental involvement in the education of children improves the well-being of families, enhances parenting skills, and improves educational results for children (Bakken & Obiakor, 2008). As such, IDEA requires parental participation in the identification and assessment processes. Culturally diverse parents must be provided with information to ensure that they understand the special education placement proceedings and decisions. In the event that the parents speak English as a second language, an option may be to give parents the materials in English as well as have them translated into their native language so that they have a better chance of understanding the information and process.

To achieve effective collaboration with CLD families and students with disabilities, their feelings must be acknowledged. School personnel must be actively engaged in building trust with the CLD families they serve. Determining how to build trust can be a complex task, but it doesn't have to be; in many ways, it is the extension of common courtesies that one would expect in any relationship. School staff members should remember the mantra to treat others as you would want to be treated. Parents have identified frequent, open, and honest communication as a primary factor in creating a positive partnership with teachers and schools (Blue-Banning, Summers, Frankland, Nelson, & Beegle, 2004). Similarly, parents would like education professionals to be forthright about issues of concern with their child but to frame it in a manner that does not place blame and is sensitive to the fact that it is their child being discussed (Blue-Banning et al., 2004). Parents want to be contacted immediately when a problem arises so that they can be involved and help deal with it. Finally, parents expressed contempt toward service providers who do not disclose information about available resources (Blue-Banning et al., 2004).

Parents also want to hear of the successes with their child and what is going well. It seems that many times parents are only contacted when there is a problem or something is wrong, which helps to promote a negative association with teachers and schools. By being positive and sharing students' progress and success with parents, the parents will begin to understand that there will be ups and downs throughout the learning process. There are many contextual factors related to trust, which is a necessary element for enabling effective collaboration with CLD families and students with disabilities. These procedures will go a long way from elementary school through to high school when students and families are considering the next steps for their education. It is very apparent that to make a successful educational plan for a CLD student with a disability, general and special educators must include the student as well as his or her family and consider the family's cultural values to the best of their abilities.

Involving Families in the Life of the School

Another aspect to improving communication is to be observant. Lindstrom et al. (2007) recommended that special educators and other professionals listen more, observe family communication patterns, slow down, be aware of nonverbal behaviors or gestures, and consult cultural guides or mediators when interacting with members of various CLD groups. Educators should learn about the students, their families, their cultures and traditions, what is important to them, and their views on education. This inquisitive attitude and the information gained will only help increase the involvement and collaboration of families.

CONCLUSION

It is difficult to find an overarching theme that adequately describes all or even some of the views on collaboration with parents and families of individuals with disabilities; however, communication issues tend to be a leading factor. One thing is for sure, collaboration is essential for the growth and development of the child with disabilities. Some parents are very involved, some are overly involved, and yet some are only a little or not involved at all with the education of their child with disabilities. Parents of individuals with disabilities are often inadequately prepared to deal with the challenges their children with disabilities present to them.

The uneven provision of services for individuals with disabilities presents another issue for families. It is more likely that adequate services for individuals with disabilities are available in more affluent communities. Additionally, more affluent families are better able to offset inadequate services by seeking and paying for such services privately. Culturally and linguistically diverse families, however, are less likely to live in communities with adequate services for individuals with disabilities and also less likely to be able to individually pursue such services because of their cost or unavailability. Different families have different circumstances related to language, culture, and economic security. These particular issues often take precedence over the difficulties faced by their children with disabilities and make it more difficult for them to obtain existing services. The inability of some teachers and schools to interact in a supportive manner adds to the barriers families may be experiencing.

Given the stress that individuals with disabilities can place on their parents, much of the intervention research seeks to treat the family unit as a whole. A variety of cultural and economic factors influence the nature and effectiveness of family treatment, but it is clear that families are best considered as important members of treatment teams for individuals with disabilities.

Finally, teachers and other school officials can work to improve their interactions with families of individuals with disabilities. Educators are in a unique position to assist families in supporting their children with disabilities but also face a number of competing requirements such as standards-based curricular initiatives and lack of resources themselves. The underlying message, however, is that teachers and schools need to collaborate with parents, communicate effectively and efficiently in a language that the parents can understand, and value parental insight and input. As we pursue the goals of educating and caring for individuals with disabilities, researchers and policy makers can enhance efforts by ensuring the adequacy of basic services for individuals with disabilities and also by continuing to pursue a more complete and clear understanding of different cultures and values and how they impact children's learning.

14

Response to Intervention and the Inclusive Classroom Teacher

In today's schools, there has been a change from immediately referring students with potential disabilities for special education services when a deficiency appears to implementing evidence-based strategies and data collection in the classroom. This process is referred to as Response to Intervention (RtI). Upon implementing strategies, teachers collect data on the progress the student is making (or lack of it) for at least 6–8 weeks. It is important that general education teachers investigate the progress students are making and how they can impact student's learning prior to referral for special education. Brigham and Brigham (2010) noted that RtI was developed through special education research in an effort to

- increase the accuracy of eligibility decisions for special education,
- prevent students without disabilities from falling so far behind that they require special education,
- focus instructional attention on standards-based curricula, and
- improve the professionalism of educational decision making.

Behind RtI is the idea that screening every child regularly on simple performance indicators that are critically related to important curricular outcomes gives general education teachers knowledge of their students' learning and data that indicates where students are showing signs of difficulty. This information allows them to provide students with modest levels of support before their instructional problems become insurmountable. This approach is more proactive and is in contrast to the reactive approach that most schools have seemed to incorporate, where if students failed or were behind, it was their problem.

The Importance of RtI for Inclusive Classroom Teachers

An effective inclusive classroom teacher faces many different challenges. The teacher might be involved in planning, delivering, and assessing instruction for a wide variety of students in his or her classroom. The ability to meet the individual needs of every student in the classroom is a top priority for inclusive classroom teachers, and RtI can help. Frequent and consistent student assessments, collecting and monitoring data on student progress, evidence-based strategies, and meaningful decision making help inclusive classroom teachers improve themselves as teachers and meet the needs of students in the classroom. For those students having difficulties, RtI provides data to support instructional changes and offers individual students the instructional support they need to be successful. Teachers are able to monitor student performance and decide if the evidence-based interventions chosen have been effective for their students or not. This process can also help teachers and schools keep from placing students in special education when those students are able to function in the general education classroom with instructional support from the teacher.

RtI Defined

RtI is a school-based, multitiered system that focuses on both academic and social behavior support and uses data-based decision making to match students with appropriate levels of evidence-based academic and social behavioral supports (Cates, Blum, & Swerdlik, 2011; National Association of State Directors of Special Education, 2005). RtI emphasizes the systematic collection, analysis, interpretation, and utilization of data to match student levels of academic functioning and social behavior with appropriate instruction and intervention. The goal of the RtI model is to help teachers identify students' academic and social needs at the onset of difficulties before they get too extreme and to prevent problems in school from intensifying. See Figures 14–17 for depictions of RtI in visual form.

RtI is comprised of three tiers that work together to address the learning and social needs of all students. In Tier 1 (universal core), the needs of at least 80% of the student body should be met. All students should receive instruction in Tier 1,

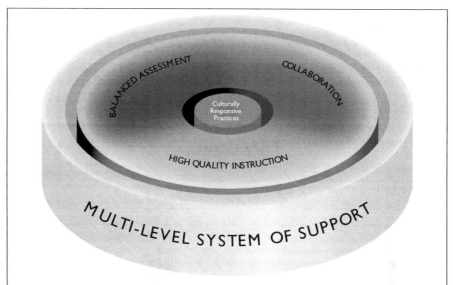

Figure 14. Visual depiction of RtI: Wisconsin's vision for RtI. From "State RtI Models for Gifted Children" by K. Rollins, C. V. Mursky, and S. K. Johnsen, In *RtI for Gifted Students* (p. 25) edited by M. R. Coleman and S. K. Johnsen, 2011, Waco, TX: Prufrock Press. Copyright 2011 Prufrock Press. Reprinted with permission.

and teachers should implement strategies that are evidence-based and supported by research to improve learning. There are two goals for the assessment process in Tier 1. First, educators should use screening measures to identify the students who are most likely to fall behind in the classroom and school. Second, schools should examine the performance of students in all academic and social areas throughout the school district. Students who are having some difficulties in Tier 1 will receive additional services in Tier 2 (small-group interventions). Students who move into Tier 2 typically receive instruction in a small-group format with interventions that have been proven to be effective through research. The goal of assessment in Tier 2 is to identify general areas of weakness for a student who is in need of further intervention and to implement an intervention that will help the student to succeed. Finally, if a student is still having a documented difficulty in Tier 2, then she should receive Tier 3 (individualized intervention) services. In addition to receiving instruction in Tiers 1 and 2, the student would also receive instruction at Tier 3. In most cases, about 5% of the students in a school building will be at the Tier 3 level. The interventions provided at this level should be evidence-based and delivered more intensively (i.e., more time, smaller group, and/or more narrow curricular focus) to meet the specific needs of the given student. The goal of assessment at Tier 3 is to address specific learning needs, improve learning, and determine if special education is needed or not.

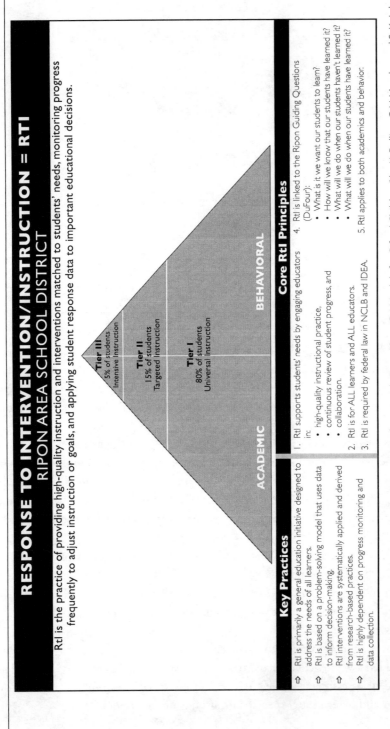

RESPONSE TO INTERVENTION/INSTRUCTION = RTI
RIPON AREA SCHOOL DISTRICT

RtI is the practice of providing high-quality instruction and interventions matched to students' needs, monitoring progress frequently to adjust instruction or goals, and applying student response data to important educational decisions.

Tier III
5% of students
Intensive Instruction

Tier II
15% of students
Targeted Instruction

Tier I
80% of students
Universal Instruction

ACADEMIC   BEHAVIORAL

Key Practices

⇨ RtI is primarily a general education initiative designed to address the needs of all learners.
⇨ RtI is based on a problem-solving model that uses data to inform decision-making.
⇨ RtI interventions are systematically applied and derived from research-based practices.
⇨ RtI is highly dependent on progress monitoring and data collection.

Core RtI Principles

1. RtI supports students' needs by engaging educators in:
   • high-quality instructional practice,
   • continuous review of student progress, and
   • collaboration.
2. RtI is for ALL learners and ALL educators.
3. RtI is required by federal law in NCLB and IDEA.
4. RtI is linked to the Ripon Guiding Questions (DuFour):
   • What is it we want our students to learn?
   • How will we know that our students have learned it?
   • What will we do when our students haven't learned it?
   • What will we do when our students have learned it?
5. RtI applies to both academics and behavior.

Figure 15. *Visual depiction of RtI: Ripon Area School District RtI framework.* From "State RtI Models for Gifted Children" by K. Rollins, C. V. Mursky, and S. K. Johnsen. In *RtI for Gifted Students* (p. 33) edited by M. R. Coleman and S. K. Johnsen, 2011, Waco, TX: Prufrock Press. Copyright 2011 Prufrock Press. Reprinted with permission.

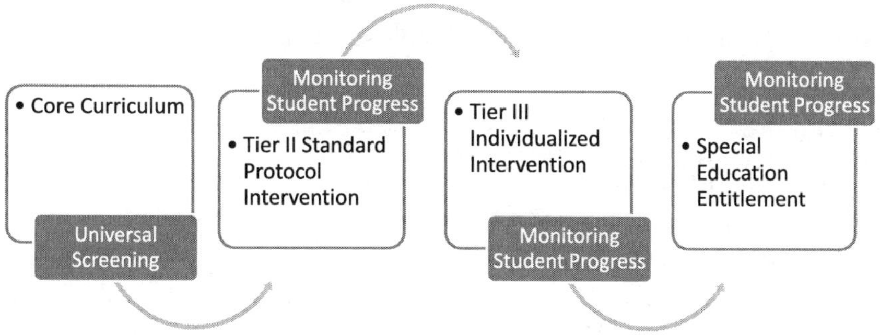

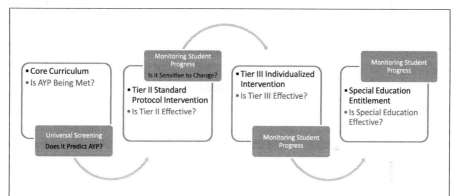

Figure 16. Visual depiction of RtI: Common components in a Response to Intervention model. From "Data-Based Decision Making Across a Multitiered System of Support" by G. L. Cates, In *Response to Intervention in the Core Content Areas* (p. 263) edited by J. P. Bakken, 2012, Waco, TX: Prufrock Press. Copyright 2012 Prufrock Press. Reprinted with permission.

Figure 17. Visual depiction of RtI: Standard questions to be answered in an RtI model. From "Data-Based Decision Making Across a Multitiered System of Support" by G. L. Cates, In *Response to Intervention in the Core Content Areas* (p. 263) edited by J. P. Bakken, 2012, Waco, TX: Prufrock Press. Copyright 2012 Prufrock Press. Reprinted with permission.

Why Implement RtI?

There are four major reasons for implementing an RtI framework. First, data-based decision making is emphasized. Educators must be accustomed to investigating a variety of data on their students so that they can make accurate decisions related to their instructional practices (e.g. Cates et al., 2003). Second, the RtI framework emphasizes evidence-based practices. An RtI framework can help ensure that schools are administering effective instructional practices with high educational standards to all of their students. Third, unlike more traditional school service delivery models that tend to exclude some students, RtI focuses on the learning of all students. Fourth, although no federal mandate (including NCLB or IDEA) currently has been proposed to enforce an RtI model of educational service delivery, all states have seen the benefits of an RtI system of delivery and are implementing some form of RtI policy (Derby, 2011).

Evidence-Based Practices

The use of data helps to establish and create evidence-based practices (EBP). EBP involves using effective and efficient educational practices through different tiers of instruction with students having difficulties with their learning based on their respective educational needs, thus minimizing learning and social behavioral concerns because interventions are chosen individually for each group of students or for each specific student. EBPs are implemented in a very systematic way by specifically targeting the learning or behavioral problems that are demonstrated to be problematic (through the collection of data) by the student and focusing on improvement and monitoring through constant assessment.

Empirical Support for RtI

The truth of the matter is that empirically supported strategies can often take years before they are used in the school system by teachers. On the other hand, practices that have little to no empirical support often make their ways into the school systems (e.g., focusing on learning styles; see Kavale & Forness, 1987). Many times teachers implement interventions that they "think" will be effective based on their own or other's teaching experiences. Fortunately, RtI has a multitude of empirical research support, including curriculum-based measurement (CBM, Deno, 1985), behavioral consultation (Bergan & Kratochwill, 1990), and Positive Behavioral Intervention Support (PBIS; Sugai & Horner, 2006).

CBM is a major component of RtI, as it allows for all students to be regularly assessed in a way that is highly effective and efficient. Students' scores from these assessments represent their understanding of the curriculum that they are exposed to on a daily basis. The benchmarking and progress monitoring activities prevalent in most RtI models today are based on the idea of CBM. The adaption of interventions and changing and modifying the specific processes (Bergan & Kratochwill, 1990) to students to help them be more successful is prevalent in the RtI framework. In addition, focusing on an individual's behavior was introduced by Sugai and Horner's (2006) Positive Behavior Intervention Support system. This three-tiered system was the basis for RtI and is the general framework for RtI as we know it today. Gresham (1991) looked at specific individuals who were struggling in schools and pioneered the concept of identifying possible students for special education based on their responsiveness to interventions. If students responded positively to interventions, then where and how they were being educated was fine; if they did not respond appropriately to interventions, then special education was an option.

Using Data to Make Decisions

In the past, educators made many decisions according to anecdotal and arbitrary information, feelings of school staff, and teacher and administrator beliefs. RtI can help minimize this practice through the use of continuous data collection, analysis, and implementation of evidence-based strategies that have been proven effective with students. Schools implementing RtI are continuously screening and monitoring student performance in addition to collecting diagnostic data and evaluating the overall program.

Implementing Best Practices

Although RtI has been present in many states for many years, it has only recently started to emerge as a comprehensive model for school systems throughout the nation (Burns & Gibbons, 2008). Prior to using RtI, schools implemented a more traditional model of service delivery (based on the medical model), generally providing services to students who performed poorly on academic tests. Students needed to demonstrate a severe discrepancy from their age-level peers on achievement tests or a severe discrepancy between their own cognitive ability and their respective level of academic performance in order to receive help and services. Although this may seem like a reasonable approach for allocating services and resources to students, it can create many problems.

First, the traditional model focuses on students who are referred by an adult who believes that the student is struggling as compared to her peers. In contrast, a hallmark of RtI is universal screening for academic and social behavioral deficits of all students relative to their peers or standards-based criteria.

Second, traditional forms of assessment involve lots of time and resources, requiring numerous hours of assessment and report writing. Frequently the information obtained is too general to help the teachers involved in the analysis. These assessments tend to be a poor use of time, and often it is hard for the assessors to keep up with which assessments need to be conducted. The backlog often causes the assessment process to not be as important as it should be, and getting the job done becomes more important than the data obtained. Implementing RtI, however, only requires a few minutes of assessment per student and, thus, is more efficient and effective. Moreover, many of the brief screening assessments can be administered in a group format, saving additional time and personnel resources.

Third, commercial instruments are often used in traditional models. In these cases, student performance is assessed against a representative national sample with little regard to the actual curriculum a student may be exposed to. As a result, the assessment data might not indicate what content the student knows or is having problems learning. RtI, on the other hand, supports the development of instruments that assess the student's actual understanding of the curriculum he has been exposed to.

Finally, and perhaps the largest concern, to meet the criteria for services under the traditional model, teachers and schools need to wait for the student to fail or be severely discrepant in academics in relation to their peers. Unfortunately, implementing services at this time can be too late and create more problems for the student. In the RtI model, screenings of academic and social behavior occurs multiple times per year, which allows educators to detect learning issues much earlier than in a traditional model. Students then receive help in a much more timely manner instead of falling grade levels behind.

CONCLUSION

Response to Intervention is a school-based approach that incorporates three distinct levels in a multitiered framework that work in unison with each other to impact the learning of all students in the classroom and school. This system involves the systematic collection, analysis, interpretation, and utilization of data to match students with the appropriate, unique academic and behavioral intervention(s) they may need. RtI is a model aimed at identifying the needs of students early on and addressing those needs before they intensify.

IF YOU WANT TO KNOW MORE

Bakken, J. P. (Ed.). (2012). *Response to intervention in the core content areas: A practical approach for educators*. Waco, TX: Prufrock Press.

Glossary

Accessibility: Actively and meaningfully included in all facilities, services, and programs. It means being able to use materials and technology that are available to other students.

Accessible text: Text that can be either transformed or manipulated into a format other than traditional print; is commonly called digital text or eText for students with disabilities.

Accommodations: Alterations to curriculum, environment, instruction, and/or materials to meet the needs of students with disabilities in the general education classroom. Accommodations do not change the standard that the student is to achieve.

Adaptive physical educators: Teachers who are specifically trained in adapting physical education instruction and activities for children with disabilities.

Aided communication: The use of tools or equipment in addition to the child's body.

American Sign Language: The preferred sign language system within the American deaf community.

Applied Behavior Analysis (ABA): Methodology based on the principle that behaviors can be changed by modifying the child's environment.

Assistive technology device: "Any item, piece of equipment, or product system, whether acquired commercially off the shelf, modified, or customized, that is used to increase, maintain, or improve the functional capabilities of a child with a disability" (IDEA, 2004, Section 300.5).

Assistive technology service: "Any service that directly assists an individual in the selection, acquisition, or use of an assistive technology device" (Tech Act, 1988).

Augmentative and alternative communication (AAC): The use of a technological device or system that is in addition to or in lieu of verbal communication.

Behavior intervention plans (BIP): Plans that are developed to meet the social, emotional, academic, behavioral, and transition needs of the individual students with challenges. The BIP identifies which behaviors will be increased, decreased, and maintained.

Board Certified Behavior Analysts (BCBA): Individuals who have specific training and skills in applying Applied Behavior Analysis techniques.

Comprehension: An active process during reading that enables the child to gain meaning from the words being read.

Computer-assisted instruction (CAI): "Computer programs that provide drill-and-practice, tutorial, or simulation activities offered either by themselves or as supplements to traditional, teacher-directed instruction" (Cotton, 1991, p. 2).

Coteaching: An educational approach in which general and special education teachers work in a coordinated fashion to jointly teach heterogeneous groups of students in educationally integrated settings.

Daily living skills: These skills facilitate a person's ability to live, work, and be involved in recreational activities in the community environment.

Education for All Handicapped Children Act (EAHCA): The first law that guaranteed students with disabilities a right to a free and appropriate public education. It was renamed as the Individuals with Disabilities Education Improvement Act (IDEA) in 1990.

Executive functioning: The ability to plan, organize, control impulses, and complete tasks.

Explicit instruction: Teacher-centered, direct instruction; the teacher decides what to teach, the objectives are clear, and students are explicitly taught concepts and skills.

Family-centered approaches: A model in which professionals actively encourage families to be involved in developing programs for their children.

FM systems: An assistive technology device that helps the student who has a hearing impairment hear his or her teacher. FM systems include a cordless microphone for teachers and receivers that attach to the student's hearing aids.

Functional behavior assessment (FBA): The process of gathering and analyzing information about a student's behavior and accompanying circumstances in order to determine the purpose or intent of the actions.

Graphic organizers: Graphic organizers combine the linguistic mode (words and phrases) and the nonlinguistic mode in that they use symbols and arrows to represent relationships among ideas.

Least restrictive environment (LRE): The LRE requires schools to educate children with disabilities as much as possible with their typically developing peers. This environment will vary based on the needs of the individual child.

Mnemonic strategy instruction: A methodology that links new information with prior knowledge using visual and auditory cues; useful for learning and remembering information.

Modifications: Modifications change the learning standard and require a different method or degree of performance but are still based on general education grade-level standards.

Orientation and Mobility Specialists (O&M): Professionals who are specifically trained to teach individuals with visual impairments or who may be blind to navigate their environments.

Phoneme awareness: The ability to recognize and manipulate the smallest units of sound, phonemes.

Phonics: The system of teaching the relationships between letters and sounds in language.

Phonological awareness: A child's ability to recognize and manipulate phonemes, syllables, and words.

Positive Behavior Intervention Supports (PBIS): Supports that are developed for the whole group while also allowing a range of increasing amounts of intervention to take place based on student need and response.

Reading fluency: The ability to read quickly and accurately.

Repeated readings: Repeated readings require students to read aloud short, meaningful passages several times while being monitored by a teacher. Students read and reread a text a certain number of times or until a certain level of fluency is reached.

Response to Intervention (RtI): School-based, multitiered system that focuses on both academic and social behavior support and uses data-based decision making to match students with appropriate levels of evidence-based academic and social behavioral supports.

Self-management: The ability to manage and evaluate one's behavior. Primary components of self-management include self-monitoring, self-observation, self-recording, self-evaluation, and self-reinforcement.

Self-regulation: The ability to monitor and self-manage one's behavior and interactions within the learning environment.

Social stories: Individualized stories that describe a specific social situation a student with disabilities may find challenging, explain the reactions of others to the situation, and provide examples of appropriate social responses.

Supported eText: Digital or electronic text supplemented with rewording, description, medial highlighted text, or other strategies to increase comprehension of material.

Text-to-speech software: Software that provides computer-synthesized speech to read digital texts to students. Text-to-speech software allows students to hear and read a text selection.

Universal Design for Learning (UDL): A model of learning that leads to the development of flexible instructional techniques and curriculum that can support all learners more efficiently. UDL requires that teachers consider all students when designing classroom activities and lessons.

Video modeling: A strategy involving the use of videos to provide modeling of targeted skills. Videos that include the participant and videos of others have been found effective in teaching skills.

References

Allor, J. H., Mathes, P. G., Champlin, T., & Cheatham, J. P. (2009). Research-based techniques for teaching early reading skills to students with intellectual disabilities. *Education and Training in Developmental Disabilities, 44*, 356–366.

Allor, J. H., Mathes, P. G., Jones, F. G., Champlin, T. M., & Cheatham, J. P. (2010). Individualized research based reading instruction for students with intellectual disabilities: Success stories. *TEACHING Exceptional Children, 42*(3), 6–12.

American Association on Intellectual and Developmental Disabilities. (2013). *Definition of intellectual disability.* Retrieved from http://www.aaidd.org/content_100.cfm

American Speech-Language-Hearing Association. (n.d.). *Augmentative and alternative communication.* Retrieved from http://www.asha.org/public/speech/disorders/AAC.htm

Americans with Disabilities Act, 42 U.S.C. §§ 12102 et seq. (1990).

Anderson-Inman, L. (2009). Supported eText: Literacy scaffolding for students with disabilities. *Journal of Special Education Technology, 24*(3), 1–7.

Anderson-Inman, L., & Horney, M. (1998). Transforming text for at-risk readers. In D. Reinking, L. Labbo, M. McKenna, & R. Kieffer (Eds.), *Handbook of literacy and technology: Transformations in a post-typographic world* (pp. 15–43). Mahwah, NJ: Lawrence Erlbaum.

Anderson-Inman, L., & Horney, M. (2007). Supported eText: Assistive technology through text transformations. *Reading Research Quarterly, 42,* 153–160.

Armbruster, B. B., Lehr, F., & Osborn, J., (2001). *Put reading first—The research building blocks for teaching children to read.* Retrieved from http://www.nichd.nih.gov/publications/pubs/PRF-teachers-k-3.cfm

Bakken, J. P. (2012). *Response to intervention in the core content areas: A practical approach for educators.* Waco, TX: Prufrock Press.

Bakken, J. P., Mastropieri, M. A., & Scruggs, T. E. (1997). Reading comprehension of expository science material and students with learning disabilities: A comparison of strategies. *Journal of Special Education, 31,* 300–324.

Bauer, A. M., Keefe, C. H., & Shea, T. M. (2001). *Students with learning disabilities or emotional/behavioral disorders.* Upper Saddle River, NJ: Prentice-Hall, Inc.

Baumrind, D. (1967). Child care practices anteceding three patterns of preschool behavior. *Genetic Psychology Monographs, 75*(1), 43–88.

Bauwens, J., Hourcade, J. J., & Friend, M. (1989). Cooperative teaching: A model for general and special education integration. *Remedial and Special Education, 10,* 17–22.

Behrmann, M., & Jerome, M. K. (2002). Assistive technology for students with mild disabilities: Update 2002. *ERIC Digest.* Retrieved from http://www.ericdigests.org/2003-1/assistive.htm

Behrmann, M., & Schaff, J. (2001). Assisting educators with assistive technology: Enabling children to achieve independence in living and learning. *Children and Families, 42*(3), 24–28.

Bergan, J. R., & Kratochwill, T. R. (1990). *Behavioral consultation and therapy.* New York, NY: Plenum.

Bethell, S. C., & Miller, N. B. (1998). From an E to an A in first-year algebra with the help of a graphing calculator. *Mathematics Teacher, 91,* 118–119.

Biederman, J., Faranone, S. V., Keenan, K., Benjamin, J., Krifcher, B., Moore, C., . . . & Steingard, R. (1992). Further evidence for family-genetic risk factors in attention deficit hyperactivity disorder. *Archives of General Psychiatry, 48,* 633–642.

Blachman, B. (1991). Early intervention for children's reading problems: Clinical applications of the research in phonological awareness. *Topics in Language Disorders, 12,* 51–65.

Blackhurst, A. E. (1997). Perspectives on technology in special education. *Teaching Exceptional Children, 29*(5), 41–48.

Blair, R. B., Ormsbee, C., & Brandes, J. (2002). *Using writing strategies and visual thinking software to enhance the written performance of students with mild disabilities.* Retrieved from http://www.eric.ed.gov/PDFS/ED463125.pdf

Blue-Banning, M., Summers, J. A., Frankland, H. C., Nelson, L. L., & Beegle, G. (2004). Dimensions of family and professional partnerships: Constructive guidelines for collaboration. *Exceptional Children, 70,* 167–184.

Bock, S. J., Bakken, J. P., Kempel-Michalak, N. (2009). Behavioral interventions for children and youth with autism spectrum disorders. In V. G. Spencer & C. G. Simpson (Eds.), *Teaching children with autism in the general classroom* (pp. 109–141). Waco, TX: Prufrock Press.

Boone, R., & Higgins, K. (2007). The role of instructional design in assistive technology research and development. *Reading Research Quarterly, 42,* 135–140.

Bouck, E. C. (2010). Technology and students with disabilities: Does it solve all the problems? In F. E. Obiakor, J. P. Bakken, & A. F. Rotatori (Eds.). *Advances in special education: Current issues and trends in special education research, technology, and teacher preparation* (Vol. 20, pp. 91–106). Bingley, England: Emerald Group Publishing.

Bouck, E. C., & Flanagan, S. M. (2009). Assistive technology and mathematics: What is there and where can we go in special education? *Journal of Special Education Technology, 24,* 17–30.

Bouck, E. C., & Flanagan, S. M. (2010). Virtual manipulatives: What they are and how teachers can use them. *Intervention in School and Clinic, 45,* 186–191.

Bouck, E. C., Joshi, G. S., & Johnson, L. (in press). Calculating the value of calculators: Who uses them and do they help? *Educational Studies in Mathematics.*

Bouck, E. C., Shurr, J. C., Tom, K., Jasper, A. D., Bassette, L., Miller, B., & Flanagan, S. M. (2012). Fix it with TAPE: Repurposing technology to be assistive technology for students with high-incidence disabilities. *Preventing School Failure, 56,* 121–128.

Bowen, S. K., & Rude, H. A. (2006). Assessment and students with disabilities: Issues and challenges with educational reform. *Rural Special Education Quarterly, 25*(3), 24–30.

Boyd, B. A., & Correa, V. I. (2005). Developing a framework for reducing the cultural clash between African American parents and the special education system. *Multicultural Perspectives, 7,* 3–11.

Brigham, F. J., & Brigham, M. S. P. (2010). Preventive instruction: Response to intervention can catch students before their problems become insurmountable. *The American School Board Journal, 197*(6), 32–33.

Bryant, D. P., & Bryant, B. R. (2003). *Assistive technology for people with disabilities.* Boston, MA: Allyn & Bacon.

Bryant, D. P., Young, S., & Dickson, C. (2001). Secondary level students with reading disabilities: No time to waste. *LDA Newsbriefs, 36*(1), 12–13, 20.

Burgstahler, S. (2003). *DO-IT: Helping students with disabilities transition to college and careers.* Minneapolis, MN: National Center on Secondary Education and Transition. Retrieved from http://www.ncset.org/publications/viewdesc.asp?id=1168

Burns, M. K., & Gibbons, K. (2008). *Response to intervention implementation in elementary and secondary schools: Procedures to assure scientific-based practices.* New York, NY: Routledge.

Carey, W. B. (2009). Normal individual differences in temperament and behavioral adjustment. In W. B. Carey, A. C. Crocker, W. L. Coleman, E. R. Elias, & H. M. Feldman (Eds.), *Developmental-behavioral pediatrics* (4th ed., pp. 74–86). Philadelphia, PA: Saunders/Elsevier.

Carter, E. W., Sisco, L. G., Chung, Y. C., & Stanton-Chapman, T. L. (2010). Peer interactions of students with intellectual disabilities and/or autism: A map of the intervention literature. *Research & Practice for Persons with Severe Disabilities, 35*(3–4), 63–79.

Cass, M., Cates, D., Smith, M., & Jackson, C. (2003). Effects of manipulative instruction on solving area and perimeter problems by students with learning disabilities. *Learning Disabilities Research & Practice, 18,* 112–120.

Cates, G. L., Blum, C., & Swerdlik, M. E. (2011). *Effective RTI training and practices: Helping school and district teams improve academic performance and social behavior.* Champaign, IL: Research Press.

Cates, G. L., Skinner, C. H., Watson, T. S., Smith, T. L., Weaver, A., & Jackson, B. (2003). Instructional effectiveness and instructional efficiency as considerations for data-based decision making: An evaluation of interspersing procedures. *School Psychology Review,* 601–616.

Chess, S., & Thomas, A. (1996). *Temperament: Theory and practice.* New York, NY: Brunner/Mazel.

Christ, T. (2008). Technology support services in postsecondary education: A mixed methods study. *Technology & Disability, 20*(1), 25–35.

Clark, J. G. (1981). Uses and abuses of hearing loss classification. *Asha, 23,* 493–500.

Cook, B. G., Shepherd, K. G., Cook, S. C., & Cook, L. (2012). Facilitating the effective implementation of evidence-based practices through teacher-parent collaboration. *Teaching Exceptional Children, 44,* 22–30.

Cooper, C. (2009). Parent involvement, African American mothers, and the politics of educational care. *Equity & Excellence in Education, 42,* 379–394.

Correa, V., Jones, H., Thomas, C., & Morsink, C., (2005). *Interactive teaming: Enhancing programs for students with special needs* (4th ed.). Upper Saddle River, NJ: Pearson.

Cotton, K. (1991). Computer-assisted instruction. *School improvement research series: Close-up #10.* Retrieved from http://www.nwrel.org/scpd/sirs/5/cu10.html

Courtad, C. A. (2011). Assistive technology specialist. In C. G. Simpson & J. P. Bakken (Eds.), *Collaboration: A multidisciplinary approach to educating students with disabilities* (pp. 183–192). Waco, TX: Prufrock Press.

Cox, J. E., & Lynch, D. M. (2006). Library media centers: Accessibility in rural Missouri. *Intervention in School and Clinic, 42*(2), 101–106.

Crosnoe, R. (2001). Academic orientation and parental involvement in education during high school. *Sociology of Education, 74,* 210–230.

Davis, M. R., Culotta, V. P., Levine, E. A., & Rice, E. H. (2011). *School success for kids with emotional and behavioral disorders.* Waco, TX: Prufrock Press.

deBettencourt, L. U. (2002). Understanding differences between IDEA and Section 504. *TEACHING Exceptional Children, 34*(3), 16–23.

Dehn, M. J. (2006). *Essentials of processing assessment.* Hoboken, NJ: John Wiley & Sons.

Delano, M. E. (2007). Video modeling interventions for individuals with autism. *Remedial and Special Education, 28*(1), 33–42.

Deno, S. L. (1985). Curriculum-based measurement: The emerging alternative. *Exceptional Children, 52,* 219–232.

Derby, K. (2011). *The status of state-level response to intervention policies and procedures in the west region states and five other states.* Retrieved from http://www.wested.org/cs/we/view/rstudy/56

Doll, B., Spies, R. A., LeClair, C. M., Kurien, S. A., & Foley, B. P. (2010). Student perceptions of classroom learning environments: Development of the classmaps survey. *School Psychology Review, 39,* 203–218.

Douglas, K. H., Ayres, K. M., Langone, J., Bell, V., & Meade, C. (2009). Expanding literacy for learners with intellectual disabilities: The role of supported eText. *Journal of Special Education Technology, 24*(3), 35–44.

Dove, M. K. (2012). Advancements in assistive technology and AT laws for the disabled. *The Delta Kappa Gamma Bulletin, 78*(4), 23–29.

Education for All Handicapped Children Act of 1975, Pub. Law 94-142 (November 29, 1975).

Edyburn, D. L. (2000). Assistive technology and students with mild disabilities. *Focus on Exceptional Children, 32*(9), 1–24.

Edyburn, D. L. (2001). Models, theories, and frameworks: Contributions to understanding special education technology. *Special Education Technology Practice, 4*(2), 16–24. Retrieved from http://cte.jhu.edu/accessibility/primer/resources/data/assistivetech/brochure_edy_burn.pdf

Edyburn, D. L. (2005). Assistive technology and students with mild disabilities: From consideration to outcomes measurement. In D. Edyburn, K. Higgins, & R. Boone (Eds.), *Handbook of special education technology research and practice* (pp. 239–270). Whitefish Bay, WI: Knowledge by Design.

Edyburn, D. L., Higgins, K., & Boone, R. (Eds.). (2005). *Handbook of special education technology research and practice.* Whitefish Bay, WI: Knowledge by Design.

Elementary and Secondary Education Act of 1969, §142, 20 U.S.C. 863.

Ellington, A. (2003). A meta-analysis of the effects of calculators on students' achievement and attitude levels in precollege mathematics classes. *Journal for Research in Mathematics Education, 34,* 433–463.

Ellis, E. (1991). *SLANT: A starter strategy for class participation.* Lawrence, KS: Edge Enterprises.

Ellis, E. (1992). *The LINCS vocabulary strategy.* Lawrence, KS: Edge Enterprises.

Erickson, K. A., Koppenhaver, D. A., & Cunningham, J. W. (2006). Balanced reading intervention and assessment in augmentative communication. In R. J. McCauley & M. E. Fey (Eds.), *Treatment of language disorders in children* (pp. 309–346). Baltimore, MD: Paul H. Brookes Publishing.

Farley, C., Torres, C., Wailehua, C. T., & Cook, L. (2012). Evidence-based practices for students with emotional and behavioral disorders: Improving academic achievement. *Beyond Behavior, 21*(2), 37–43.

Fitzgerald, G., & Koury, K. (2001–2002). *The KidTools support system* (Project #H327A000005). Washington, DC: U.S. Department of Education, Office of Special Education Programs.

Fitzgerald, G., & Koury, K. (2004-2005). *The strategy tools support system* (Project #H327A000005). Washington, DC: U.S. Department of Education, Office of Special Education Programs.

Friend, M., & Cook, L. (2004). *Interactions: Collaboration skills for school professionals* (5th ed.). Boston, MA: Allyn & Bacon.

Ganz, J. B, Vollrath, T. E., & Cook, K. E. (2011). Video modeling: A visually based intervention for children with autism spectrum disorder. *TEACHING Exceptional Children, 43*(6), 8–19.

Geenan, S., Powers, L. E., & Lopez-Vasquez, A. (2001). Multicultural aspects of parent involvement in transition planning. *Exceptional Children, 67,* 265–282.

Gierach, J. (Ed.). (2009). *Assessing students' needs for assistive technology* (5th ed.). Milton: Wisconsin Assistive Technology Initiative and the Wisconsin Department of Public Instruction.

Gillam, S. L., Fargo, J. D., & Robertson, K. S. C. (2009). Comprehension of expository text: Insights gained from think-aloud data. *American Journal of Speech-Language Pathology, 18,* 82–94.

Gordon, S. M., & Miller, H. L. (2003, April). Parents as active team members: Where does accountability for a child's special education rest? Paper presented at the Annual Meeting of the American Educational Research Association, Chicago, IL.

Green, R. A. (2009). Empowering library patrons with learning disabilities. *Journal of Access Services, 6,* 59–71.

Gresham, F. M. (1991). Conceptualizing behavior disorders in terms of resistance to intervention. *School Psychology Review, 20*(1), 23–36.

Gross, D., Julion, W., & Fogg, L. (2001). What motivates participation and dropout among low-income urban families of color in a prevention intervention? *Family Relations, 50,* 246–254.

Hallahan, D. P., Kauffman, J. M., & Pullen, P. C. (2012). *Exceptional learners: An introduction to special education* (12th ed.). Upper Saddle, NJ: Pearson.

Halpern, A. S. (1992). Transition: Old wine in new bottles. *Exceptional Children, 58*(3), 202–211.

Harry, B. (2002). Trends and issues in serving culturally diverse families of children with disabilities. *The Journal of Special Education, 36,* 131–138.

Hetzroni, O., & Shrieber, B. (2004). Word processing as an assistive technology tool for enhancing academic outcomes of students with writing disabilities in the general classroom. *Journal of Learning Disabilities, 37,* 143–154.

Hitchcock, C., Meyer, A., Rose, D., & Jackson, R. (2002). *Providing new access to the general curriculum: Universal design for learning, 35*(2), 8–17.

Hollingsworth, J., & Ybarra, S. (2009). *Explicit direct instruction.* Thousand Oaks, CA: Corwin Press.

Huntington, D. J. (1995). Instruction in concrete, semi-concrete, and abstract representation as an aid to the solution of relational problems by adolescents with learning disabilities. *Dissertation Abstracts International, 56,* 512.

Idol, L. (2006). Toward inclusion of special education students in general education: A program evaluation of eight schools. *Remedial and Special Education, 27*(2), 77–94.

Idol-Maestas, L. (1985). Getting ready to read: Guided probing for poor comprehenders. *Learning Disability Quarterly, 8,* 243–254.

Individuals with Disabilities Education Improvement Act, Pub. Law 108-446 (December 3, 2004).

Izzo, M., Yurick, A., & McArrell, B. (2009). Supported eText: Effects of text-to-speech on access and achievement for high school students with disabilities. *Journal of Special Education Technology, 24*(3), 9–20.

Johnson, L., Beard, L. A., & Carpenter, L. B. (2007). *Assistive technology: Access for all students.* Upper Saddle River, NJ: Pearson.

Johnson, K. L., Dudgeon, B., Kuehn, C., & Walker, W. (2007). Assistive technology use among adolescents and young adults with spina bifida. *American Journal of Public Health, 97,* 330–336.

Jordan, L., Miller, D. M., & Mercer, C. D. (1998). The effects of concrete to semi concrete to abstract instruction in the acquisition and retention of fraction concepts and skills. *Learning Disabilities: A Multidisciplinary Journal, 9,* 115–122.

Kavale, K. A., & Forness, S. R. (1987). Substance over style: Assessing the efficacy of modality testing and teaching. *Exceptional Children, 54,* 228–239.

Kim, K. H., & Turnbull, A. (2004). Transition to adulthood for students with severe intellectual disabilities: Shifting toward person-family interdependent planning. *Research & Practice for Persons With Severe Disabilities, 29*(1), 53–57.

King-Sears, M. (2006). Self-management for students with disabilities: The importance of teacher follow-up. *International Journal of Special Education, 21,* 94–108.

Klingner, J. K., Vaughn, S., Arguelles, M. E., Hughes, M. T., & Leftwich, S. A. (2004). Collaborative strategic reading: "Real-world" lessons from classroom teachers. *Remedial and Special Education, 25,* 291–302.

Kroesbergen, E. H., & Van Luit, J. E. H. (2003). Mathematics interventions for children with special educational needs: A meta-analysis. *Remedial and Special Education, 24*(2), 97–114.

Kuder, S. J. (1997). *Teaching students with language and communication disabilities.* Needham Heights, MA: Allyn & Bacon.

Lahm, E. A. (2003). Assistive technology specialists. *Remedial and Special Education, 24,* 141–153.

Lane, K. L., Eisner, S. L., Kretzer, J., Bruhn, A. L., Crnobori, M., Funke, L., . . . & Casey, A. (2009). Outcomes for functional assessment-based interventions for students with and at risk for emotional and behavioral disorders in a job-share setting. *Education and Treatment of Children, 32*(4), 573–604.

Lange, G., Sherrin, D., Carr, A., Dooley, B., Barton, V., Marshall, D., Mulligan, A., . . . & Doyle, M. (2005). Family factors associated with attention deficit hyperactivity disorder and emotional disorders in children. *Journal of Family Therapy, 27,* 76–96.

Lareau, A. (2000). *Home advantage: Social class and parental intervention in elementary education* (2nd ed.). Lanham, MD: Rowman & Littlefield.

LDOnline. (2010). *What is a learning disability?* Retrieved from http://www.ldonline.org/ldbasics/whatisld

Lerner, J., & Johns, B. (2009). *Learning disabilities and related mild disabilities: Characteristics, teaching strategies, and new directions* (11th ed.). Boston, MA: Houghton Mifflin Harcourt.

Lindstrom, L., Paskey, J., Dickinson, J., Doren, B., Zane, C., & Johnson, P. (2007). Voices from the field: Recommended transition strategies for students and school staff. *Journal for Vocational Special Needs Education, 29*(2), 4–15.

LoPresti, E., Mihailidis, A., & Kirsch, N. (2004). Assistive technology for cognitive rehabilitation: State of the art. *Neuropsychology Rehabilitation, 14,* 5–39.

Lucyshyn, J. M., Blumberg, E. R., & Kayser, A. T. (2000). Improving the quality of support to families of children with severe behavior problems in the first decade of the new millennium. *Journal of Positive Behavior Interventions, 2*(2), 113–115.

MacArthur, C. A. (2006). The effects of new technologies on writing and writing processes. In C. A. MacArthur, S. Graham, & J. Fitzgerald (Eds.), *Handbook of writing research* (pp. 248–262). New York, NY: Guilford.

MacArthur, C. A. (2009). Reflections on research on writing and technology for struggling writers. *Learning Disabilities Research & Practice, 24,* 93–103.

Maccini, P., & Gagnon, J. C. (2000). Best practices for teaching mathematics to secondary students with special needs. *Focus on Exceptional Children, 32*(5), 1–22.

Martin, J. E., Marshall, L. H., & Sale, P. (2004). A 3-year study of middle, junior high, and high school IEP meetings. *Exceptional Children, 70,* 285–297.

Marzano, R. J., Marzano, J. S., & Pickering, D. J. (2003). *Classroom management that works: Research-based strategies for every teacher.* Alexandria, VA: Association for Supervision and Curriculum Development.

Marzano, R. J., Pickering, D. J., & Pollock, J. E. (2001). *Classroom instruction that works: Research-based strategies for increasing student achievement.* Alexandria, VA: Association for Supervision and Curriculum Development.

Mason, L. H., & Hedin, L. R. (2011). Reading science text: Challenges for students with learning disabilities and considerations for teachers. *Learning Disabilities Research & Practice, 26,* 214–222.

Mastropieri, M. A., & Scruggs, T. E. (2010). *The inclusive classroom: Strategies for effective differentiated instruction* (4th ed.). Upper Saddle River, NJ: Pearson.

Mastropieri, M. A., Scruggs, T. E., Graetz, J., Fontana, J., Cole, V., & Gersen, A. (2005). Mnemonic strategies: What are they? How can I use them? And how effective are they? *Insights on Learning Disabilities, 2*(1), 1–17.

Mates, B. T. (2004). Information access for people with disabilities. *Library Technology Reports, 40*(3), 10–31.

Mather, N., & Jaffe, L. E. (2002). *Woodcock Johnson III: Reports, recommendations, and strategies.* New York, NY: John Wiley & Sons.

McGuinness, D. (2005). *Language development and learning to read: The scientific study of how language development affects reading skill.* Cambridge, MA: The MIT Press.

McLeskey, J., Rosenberg, M. S., & Westling, D. L. (2013). *Inclusion: Effective practices for all students* (2nd ed.). Upper Saddle River, NJ: Pearson.

McLeskey, J., & Waldron, N. L. (2011). Educational programs for elementary students with learning disabilities: Can they be effective and inclusive? *Learning Disabilities Practice, 26*(1), 48–57.

McMullen, R. C., Shippen, M. E., & Dangel, H. L. (2007). Middle school teachers' expectations of organizational behaviors of students with learning disabilities. *Journal of Instructional Psychology, 34,* 75–82.

Mechling, L. C., Gast, D. L., & Langone, J. (2002). Computer-based video instruction to teach persons with moderate intellectual disabilities to read grocery aisle signs and locate items. *The Journal of Special Education, 35,* 224–240.

Mercer, C. D., Mercer, A. R., & Pullen, P. C. (2011). *Teaching students with learning problems* (8th ed.). Upper Saddle River, NJ: Pearson.

Mercer, C. D., & Pullen, P. C. (2009). *Students with learning disabilities* (7th ed.). Upper Saddle River, NJ: Pearson.

Mitchem, K., Kight, J., Fitzgerald, G., & Koury, K. (2007). Electronic performance support systems: An assistive technology for secondary students with mild disabilities. *Journal of Special Education Technology, 22*(2), 1–14.

Montgomery, D. J., & Marks, L. J. (2006). Using technology to build independence in writing for students with disabilities. *Preventing School Failure, 50*(3), 33–38.

Mooney, P., Ryan, J. B., Uhing, B. M., Reid, R., & Epstein, M. H. (2005). A review of self-management interventions targeting academic outcomes for students with emotional and behavioral disorders. *Journal of Behavioral Education, 14,* 203–221.

Mueller, T. (2009). IEP facilitation: A promising approach to resolving conflicts between families and schools. *Teaching Exceptional Children, 41,* 60–67.

National Association of the Deaf. (n.d.) *American Sign Language: Access to language is a human right.* Retrieved from http://nad.org/issues/american-sign-language

National Association of State Directors of Special Education. (2005). *Response to Intervention: Policy considerations and implementation.* Alexandria, VA: Author.

National Center for Learning Disabilities. (2010). *What is executive function?* Retrieved from http://www.ncld.org/ld-basics/ld-aamp-executive-functioning/basic-ef-facts/what-is-executive-function

National Dissemination Center for Children with Disabilities. (2012). *Visual impairment, including blindness.* Retrieved from http://nichcy.org/disability/specific/visualimpairment

National Reading Panel. (2000). *Teaching children to read: An evidence-based assessment of the scientific research literature on reading and its implications for reading instruction.* Washington DC: National Institute of Child Health and Human Development/National Institutes of Health.

Neece, C., Kraemer, B., & Blacher, J. (2009). Transition satisfaction and family well being among parents of young adults with severe intellectual disability. *Intellectual and Developmental Disabilities, 47,* 31–43.

No Child Left Behind Act, 20 U.S.C. §6301 (2001).

Obiakor, F. E. (2008). *The eight-step approach to multicultural learning and teaching* (3rd ed.). Dubuque, IA: Kendall/Hunt.

Overton, T. (2009). *Assessing learners with special needs* (6th ed.). Upper Saddle River, NJ: Pearson/Merrill.

Pakulski, L. A., & Kaderavek, J. N. (2002). Children with minimal hearing loss: Intervention in the classroom. *Intervention in School and Clinic, 38,* 96–103.

Parette, H. P., Peterson-Karlan, G. R., & Wojcik, B. W. (2005). The state of assistive technology services nationally and implications for future development. *Assistive Technology Outcomes and Benefits, 2*(1), 13–24.

Pena, D. C. (2000). Parent involvement: Influencing factors and implications. *Journal of Educational Research, 94*(1), 42–54.

Perla, F., & Ducret, W. D. (1999). Guidelines for teaching orientation and mobility to children with multiple disabilities. *Re:View, 31,* 113–120.

Peterson-Karlan, G. R. (2011). Technology to support writing by students with learning and academic disabilities: Recent research trends and findings. *Assistive Technology Outcomes and Benefits, 7*(1), 39–62.

Ploessl, D. M., Rock, M., Schoenfeld, N., & Blanks, B. (2010). On the same page: Practical techniques to enhance co-teaching interactions. *Intervention in School & Clinic, 45,* 158–168.

Pugach, M. C., & Winn, J. A. (2011). Research on co-teaching and teaming: An untapped resource for induction. *Journal of Special Education Leadership, 24*(1), 17–27.

Quinn, B. S., Behrmann, M., Mastropieri, M., Bausch, M. E., Ault, M. J., & Chung, Y. (2009). Who is using assistive technology in schools? *Journal of Special Education Technology, 24*(1), 1–13.

Rademacher, J. A., Pemberton, J. B., & Cheever, G. L. (2006). *Focusing together: Promoting self-management skills in the classroom.* Lawrence, KS: Edge Enterprises.

Raver, S. (2009). *Early childhood special education—0-8 years, strategies for positive outcomes.* Upper Saddle River, NJ: Pearson.

Reid, R., & Katsiyannis, A. (1995). Attention-deficit disorder/hyperactivity disorder and Section 504. *Remedial and Special Education, 16*(1), 44–52.

Reimer, K., & Moyer, P. S. (2005). Third-graders learn about fractions using virtual manipulatives: A classroom study. *Journal of Computers in Mathematics and Science Teaching, 24*(1), 5–25.

Rollins, K., Mursky, C. V., & Johnsen, S. K. (2011). State RtI models for gifted children In M. R. Coleman & S. K. Johnsen (Eds.), *RtI for gifted students* (pp. 25–41). Waco, TX: Prufrock Press.

Rose, D. H., & Meyer, A. (2002). *Teaching every student in the digital age: Universal design for learning.* Alexandria, VA: Association for Supervision and Curriculum Development.

Rose, E., & Huefner, D. S. (1984). Cultural bias in special education assessment and placement. In T. N. Jones, & D. Semler (Eds.), *School law update: Preventive school law* (pp. 179–188). Topeka, KS: National Organization on Legal Problems of Education.

Romski, M., Sevcik, R. A., Cheslock, M., & Barton, A. (2006). The system for augmenting language. In R. J. McCauley & M. E. Fey (Eds.), *Treatment of language disorders in children* (pp. 123–147). Baltimore, MD: Paul H. Brookes Publishing.

Rueter, J. A., & Trice, J. N. (2011). From high school to juvenile corrections: The downward spiral. *The International Journal on School Disaffection, 8*(2), 34–41.

Sack-Min, J. (2007). The issues of IDEA. *American School Board Journal, 194*(3), 20–25.

Salend, S. J. (2011). *Creating inclusive classrooms: Effective and reflective practices* (7th ed.). Upper Saddle River, NJ: Pearson.

Santangelo, T., & Olinghouse, N. G. (2009). Effective writing instruction for students who have writing difficulties. *Focus on Exceptional Children, 42*(4), 1–20.

Schoenfeld, N. A., & Konopasek, D. (2007). Medicine in the classroom: A review of psychiatric medications for students with emotional or behavioral disorders. *Beyond Behavior, 17*(1), 14–20.

Schuele, C. M. (2004). The impact of developmental speech and language impairments on the acquisition of literacy skills. *Mental Retardation and Developmental Disabilities Research Reviews, 10,* 176–183.

Schmidt, C. M. (2011). Audiologist. In C. G. Simpson & J. P. Bakken (Eds.), *Collaboration: A multidisclipinary approach to educating students with disabilities* (pp. 209–224). Waco, TX: Prufrock Press.

Section 504 of the Rehabilitation Act, 29 U.S.C. Section 706 et. Seq. (1973).

Seo, Y. J., & Bryant, D. (2009). Analysis of studies of the effects of computer-assisted instruction on the mathematics performance of students with learning disabilities. *Computers & Education, 53,* 913–928.

Seo, Y. J., & Bryant, D. (2010). Multimedia CAI program for students with mathematics difficulties. *Remedial and Special Education 33* 215–225. doi:10.1177/0741932510383322.

Sharma, P., & Hannafin, M. J. (2007). Scaffolding in technology-enhanced learning environments. *Interactive Learning Environments, 15*(1), 27–46.

Shogren, K., Lang, R., Machalicek, W., Rispoli, M., & O'Reilly, M. (2010). Self-versus teacher management of behavior for elementary school students with Asperger syndrome: Impact on classroom behavior. *Journal of Positive Behavior Interventions, 13,* 87–96.

Shrieber, B., & Seifert, T. (2009). College students with learning disabilities and/or ADHD use of a handheld computer compared to convention planners. In Y. Eshet-Alkalai, A. Caspi, S. Eden, N. Geri, Y. Yair (Eds.), *Proceedings of the chairs conference on instructional technologies research 2009: Learning in the technological era.* Raanana: The Open University of Israel. Retrieved from http://telempub.openu.ac.il/users/chais/2009/noon/2_3.pdf

Simpson, C. G., Spencer, V., & Bakken, J. P. (2011). *Teacher's survival guide: The inclusive classroom.* Waco, TX: Prufrock Press.

Simpson, C. G., & Warner, L. (2010). *Successful inclusion strategies for early childhood teachers.* Waco, TX: Prufrock Press.

Simpson, R. L., LaCava, P. G., & Graner, P. (2004). The No Child Left Behind act: Challenges and implications for educators. *Intervention in School and Clinic, 40*(2), 67–75.

Singer, B., & Bashir, A. S. (1999). What are executive functions and self-regulation and what do they have to do with language-learning disorders? *Language, Speech, and Hearing Services in Schools, 30,* 265–273.

Smith, J., Stern, K., & Shatrova, Z. (2008). Factors inhibiting Hispanic parents' school involvement. *Rural Educator, 29*(2), 8–13.

Smith, S. (2010). Introduction to the special issue on technology integration. *Learning Disability Quarterly, 33,* 240–242.

Smith, T. E. C. (2001). Section 504, the ADA, and public schools. *Remedial and Special Education, 22,* 335–343.

Smith, M., & Segal, J. (2012). *ADD/ADHD parenting tips: Helping children with attention deficit disorder.* Retrieved from http://helpguide.org/mental/adhd_add_parenting_strategies.htm

Special Olympics. (2008). *What are intellectual disabilities?* Retrieved from http://www.specialolympics.org/uploadedFiles/Fact%20Sheet_Intellectual%20Disabilities.pdf

Spencer, V., Simpson, C., & Lynch, S. (2008). Using social stories to increase positive behaviors for children with autism spectrum disorder. *Intervention School and Clinic, 44,* 58–61.

Spodak, R., & Stefano, K. (2011). *Take control of ADHD: The ultimate guide for teens with ADHD.* Waco, TX: Prufrock Press.

Stahl, S. (2004). *The promise of accessible textbooks: Increased achievement for all students.* Wakefield, MA: National Center on Accessing the General Curriculum.

Steen, K., Brooks, D., & Lyon, T. (2006). The impact of virtual manipulatives on first grade geometry instruction and learning. *Journal of Computers in Mathematics and Science Teaching, 25,* 373–391.

Stockall, N. S., Dennis, L., & Miller, J. (2012). Right from the start: Universal design for preschool. *TEACHING Exceptional Children, 45*(1), 10–17.

Sturges, K. M., Cramer, E. D., Harry, B., & Klingner, J. K. (2005). Desegregated but unequal: Some paradoxes of parent involvement at Bromden Elementary. *International Journal of Educational Policy, Research, and Practice, 6*(1), 79–104.

Sugai, G., & Horner, R. (2006). A promising approach for expanding and sustaining school-wide positive behavior support. *School Psychology Review, 35,* 45–59.

Sutherland, K. S., Lewis-Palmer, T., Stichter, J., & Morgan, P. (2008). Examining the influence of teacher behavior and classroom context on the behavioral and academic outcomes for students with emotional and behavioral disorders. *The Journal of Special Education, 41,* 223–233.

Swift, S. H., Davidson, R. C., & Weems, L. J. (2008). Cortical visual impairment in children: Presentation, intervention, and prognosis in educational settings. *TEACHING Exceptional Children, 4*(5), 2–14.

Turney, K., & Kao, G. (2009). Barriers to school involvement: Are immigrant parents disadvantaged? *Journal of Educational Research, 102,* 257–271.

Turnbull, A., Turnbull, R., Erwin, E., & Soodak, L. (2006). *Families, professionals, and exceptionality* (5th ed.). Upper Saddle River, NJ: Merrill/Prentice Hall.

Turnbull, A. P., & Turnbull, R. (2000). *Families, professionals, and exceptionalities: Collaboration for empowerment.* Englewood Cliffs, NJ: Prentice Hall.

Technology-Related Assistance for Individuals with Disabilities Act, P. L. 100-407 (1988).

U. S. Department of Education. (2003). *25th annual report to Congress on the implementation of the Individuals with Disabilities Education Act.* Washington, DC: Author.

Vanderheiden, G. (1984). High and light technology approaches in the development of communication systems for the severely physically handicapped person. *Exceptional Education Quarterly, 4*(4), 40–56.

Vaughn, S., & Coleman, M. (2004). The role of mentoring in promoting use of research-based practices in reading. *Remedial and Special Education, 25*(1), 25–38.

Vaughn, S. R., Bos, C. S., & Schumm, J. S. (2011). *Teaching students who are exceptional, diverse, and at risk in the general education classroom* (5th ed.). Upper Saddle River, NJ: Pearson.

Wagner, M., Marder, C., Blackorby, J., Cameto, R., Newman, L., Levine, P., & Davies-Mercier, E. (with Chorost, M., Garza, N., Guzman, A., & Sumi, C.). (2003). *The achievements of youth with disabilities during secondary school. A report from the national longitudinal transition study-2.* Menlo Park, CA: SRI International. Retrieved from www.nlts2.org/reports/2003_11/nlts2_report_2003_11_complete.pdf

Wendling, B. J., & Mather, B. (2009). *Essentials of evidence-based academic interventions.* Hoboken, NJ: John Wiley & Sons.

Westling, D. L., & Fox, L. (2009). *Teaching students with severe disabilities* (4th ed.). Upper Saddle River, NJ: Pearson.

Wheeler, J. J., & Richey, D. D. (2010). *Behavior management: Principles and practices of positive behavior supports* (2nd ed.). Columbus, OH: Pearson.

Williams, J.-J. IV (2008). Hovering parents bully teachers: Educators report harassment from 'helicopter' caretakers. *Baltimore Sun.* Retrieved from http://articles.baltimoresun.com/2008-03-04/news/0803040003_1_parents-howard-county-teachers

Wisconsin Department of Public Instruction. (n.d.). *Services for children with an emotional behavioral disability.* Retrieved from http://sped.dpi.wi.gov/sped_ed

Wymbs, B. T., Pelham, W. E., Gnagy, E. M., Molina, S. G., Wilson, T. K., & Greenhouse, J. B. (2008). Rate and predictors of divorce among parents of youths with ADHD. *Journal of Consulting & Clinical Psychology, 76,* 735–744.

Yawn, C. D., Hill, J. M., Obiakor, F. E., Gala, D. T. D., & Neu, J. (2013). Families and students with learning disabilities. In J. P. Bakken, F. E. Obiakor, & A. F. Rotatori (Eds.), *Learning disabilities: Practice concerns and students with LD* (Advances in Special Education, Vol. 25, pp. 175–188). Bingley, England: Emerald Publishing Group.

Yell, M. L. (2006). *The law and special education* (2nd ed.). Upper Saddle River NJ: Pearson.

Yell, M. L., Ryan, J. B., Rozalski, M. E., & Katsiyannis, A. (2009). The U.S. Supreme Court and special education: 2005–2007. *TEACHING Exceptional Children, 40*(3), 68–75.

Zigmond, N. (2003). Where should students with disabilities receive special education services? Is one place better than another? *The Journal of Special Education, 37,* 193–199.

About the Authors

Cynthia Simpson, Ph.D., is currently professor and Dean of Education in the School of Education and Behavioral Sciences at Houston Baptist University and has more than 20 years of experience in the public and private sector as a preschool teacher, special education teacher, elementary teacher, educational diagnostician, and administrator. She maintains an active role in early childhood and elementary education as an educational consultant in the areas of assessment and inclusive practices. Her professional responsibilities include serving on the National Council for Accreditation of Teacher Education (NCATE)/National Association of Young Children (NAEYC) Review Panel, as well as holding the position of State Advisor to the Texas Educational Diagnostician Association. She also represents college teachers as the President for Texas Association of College Teachers. Cynthia has many publications to her credit and is a featured speaker at the international, national, and state level. Cynthia has been awarded the 2008 Susan Phillips Gorin Award, the highest honor that can be bestowed on a professional member of the Council for Exceptional Children by its student membership. Her honors also include the 2007 Katheryn Varner Award (awarded by Texas Council for Exceptional Children) and the 2009 Wilma Jo Bush Award.

Jessica A. Rueter, Ph.D., is an assistant professor at The University of Texas at Tyler in the School of Education. Dr. Rueter has 15 years of experience working in public schools. Her research interests include best practices of assessment of students with disabilities and translating assessment results into evidence-based instructional practices.

Jeffrey P. Bakken, Ph.D., is professor, Associate Provost for Research, and Dean of the Graduate School at Bradley University. He has a bachelor's degree in elementary education from the University of Wisconsin-LaCrosse and graduate degrees in the area of special education-learning disabilities from Purdue University. Dr. Bakken is a teacher, consultant, and scholar. His specific areas of interest include Response to Intervention, collaboration, transition, teacher effectiveness, assessment, learning strategies, and technology. He has written more than 125 academic publications, including books, journal articles, chapters, monographs, reports, and proceedings, and he has made over 220 presentations at local, state, regional, national, and international levels. Dr. Bakken has received the College of Education and the University Research Initiative Award, the College of Education Outstanding College Researcher Award, the College of Education Outstanding College Teacher Award, and the Outstanding University Teacher Award from Illinois State University. Additionally, he is the editor-in-chief for *Multicultural Learning and Teaching* and on the editorial boards of many scholarly publications, including *Remedial and Special Education* and *Exceptional Children*. Through his work, he has committed himself to improving teachers' knowledge and techniques as well as services for students with exceptionalities and their families.